AI Empowered

AI Empowered: Pioneering African American Entrepreneurship in the Digital Age

BY

BABU GEORGE
Alcorn State University, USA

AND

ONTARIO S. WOODEN
North Carolina Central University, USA

emerald
PUBLISHING

United Kingdom – North America – Japan – India – Malaysia – China

Emerald Publishing Limited
Emerald Publishing, Floor 5, Northspring, 21-23 Wellington Street, Leeds LS1 4DL

First edition 2025

Reprints and permissions service
Contact: www.copyright.com
Printed and bound by CPI Group (UK) Ltd, Croydon, CR0 4YY

British Library Cataloguing in Publication Data
A catalogue record for this book is available from the British Library

ISBN: 978-1-83662-817-0 (Print)
ISBN: 978-1-83662-816-3 (Online)
ISBN: 978-1-83662-818-7 (Epub)

INVESTOR IN PEOPLE

Contents

About the Authors

Babu George is a Professor of Management and International Business at Alcorn State University, USA. He holds a Ph.D. in Management, a DBA in International Business, and an Ed.S. in Higher Education Innovation and Leadership. In 2017, he completed Harvard University's Institute for Educational Management program. He has published over 300 research papers in esteemed international scholarly journals and has authored or edited several books, including *Towards Digitally Transforming Accounting and Business Processes* (2013, Springer Nature), *Progress in Green Economics* (2022, Bentham), *Mobility and Globalization* (2022, Palgrave), *Digital Transformation in Business and Society* (2020, Palgrave), *International Case Studies in the Management of Disasters* (2020, Emerald), *Strategies for Promoting Sustainable Hospitality and Tourism Services* (2020, IGI Global), and *The Changing Landscape of Global Businesses* (2019, Cambridge Scholars). His research primarily focuses on sustainability and digital transformation, particularly in the context of AI's growing influence.

Ontario S. Wooden is Provost and Vice Chancellor for Academic Affairs and Professor of Higher Education at North Carolina Central University, USA. His research interests include college choice, access, and success, higher education policy and finance, and Artificial Intelligence (AI) in higher education. He serves on the Editorial Boards for both the *Journal of Access, Retention and Inclusion in Higher Education* and the *Journal for the Study of Sports and Athletes in Education*. Dr. Wooden earned his Bachelor's degree from Albany State University (Ga.) and his Master's and Ph.D. degrees in Higher Education from Indiana University Bloomington.

Foreword

The authors, Dr. Babu George and Dr. Ontario Wooden, examine how Artificial Intelligence (AI) intersects with entrepreneurship within the African American community. This book is written as the digital age is being defined through advances in computer technology and software systems that are emerging rapidly to think like a human and perform complex tasks that simulate reasoning, human-based learning, creativity, problem-solving, and decision-making. As AI evolves as a powerful general-purpose technology like the steam engine, railroad, electricity, automobiles, and information technology, entrepreneurs aim to understand how to harness AI in many different industries in transformative ways to create new businesses. AI has the potential to help entrepreneurs enhance productivity, streamline operations, and drive innovation.[1] This book addresses the gap in understanding how AI and its benefits are accessible for all entrepreneurs. George and Wooden draw on their scholar-practitioner expertise in leading the adoption of digital innovations in higher education and other industries to engage the reader to consider frameworks, policies, and practices necessary to drive the growth of entrepreneurship among African Americans in the fast-emerging AI era. With their expertise, George and Wooden also examine the AI-entrepreneurship ecosystem in terms of the importance of the education and community networks to address the digital divide, algorithmic bias, and access to capital.

AI Empowered opens with the journey of entrepreneurship among African Americans. Recent surveys report that entrepreneurship among African Americans has grown. Pew Research reports, "In 2022, there were 194,585 U.S. firms with majority Black or African American ownership. That's up from 124,004 in 2017, according to the latest estimates from the Annual Business Survey (ABS), conducted by the U.S. Census Bureau and the National Science Foundation."[2] The report also identifies that African American entrepreneurs own businesses in the healthcare and social assistance sector as well as the professional, scientific, and technical services sector.

---

[1]King, K., & Ganguli, A. (2024, March). Impact of artificial intelligence (AI) on entrepreneurship. In *Research-to-policy collaboration written briefs*. Penn State University, Social Science Research Institute. https://evidence2impact.psu.edu/resources/impact-of-artificial-intelligence-ai-on-entrepreneurship/

[2]Leppert, R. (2025, February 12). A look at black-owned business in the U.S. *Pew Research Center*. https://www.pewresearch.org/short-reads/2025/02/12/a-look-at-black-owned-businesses-in-the-us/

The book describes how the entrepreneurial spirit of African Americans is rooted in resilience and cultural identity that has opened the door for unprecedented innovation and economic innovation in the emerging AI era. Through this journey, AI Empowered articulates how African American entrepreneurs have turned their ideas into businesses and innovations through an expansive range of time and capital consuming tasks. The case studies and examples highlight that entrepreneurship is not easy. However, AI Empowered shares how AI can help entrepreneurs with the day-to-day work of creating and building a business.

As George and Wooden walk the reader through this journey, the authors reveal that the heart African American entrepreneurship story is learning to support entrepreneurship powered by AI. AI offers the promise of improving performance and productivity for the growing number of entrepreneurs. However, organizations struggle with understanding how to utilize technology and where to find the workforce with the skill sets to use the technology. Entrepreneurs need to understand how to tailor AI systems to meet the specific needs of their businesses and customers as expectations for digital technologies continue to change. The social media era has ushered in a participation culture and new sets of expectations for access and control over information. The public is armed increasingly with information, applications, and myriads of interconnected devices along with the expectation to participate in their service experiences. Consequently, entrepreneurs must thrive with the emergence of data analytics or "big data." With each digital transaction or performance of a process, bits of vital data are collected and stored. As organizations develop large collections of data, it is vital that they leverage AI tools to transform the data into intelligence to be competitive. Organizations need to develop the resources and capabilities to take data, which can be thought of as the raw material of information, and combine it with experience, context, and insights discover and create new knowledge to create relevant products and appropriate service experiences for their businesses. AI can assist with these requirements.

The authors detail interesting ways that AI can help entrepreneurs. Understanding AI requires the entrepreneur to learn through formal and informal means by tinkering, playing around, creating, and learn by doing to create and build business in specific institutional and cultural contexts. AI, like any digital tool or information system, does not exist in social or technological isolation. Contemporary practices in AI-enabled technology management and innovation rely on entrepreneurs developing strategic management skills to meet the specific needs of their customer base. Leading scholars in strategy and innovation observe that innovation relies on information and communication technologies to focus on the individual needs of its customers. It also relies on the ability of the entrepreneur to leverage the knowledge and skill of its workforce, coordinated organizational processes interlinked internally and externally, and highly developed data analytics.[3] The entrepreneur also learns how to make decisions to determine the right investments in human capital, innovations of processes and

[3]Prahalad, C., & Krishnan, M. (2008). *The new age of innovation: Driving co-created value through global networks*. McGraw Hill.

services, and strategies to overcome uncertainty in markets, create business models, supply-chains, and financing.

For example, George and Wooden consider the importance of education and community networks to drive learning for entrepreneurs support the AI-entrepreneurship ecosystem. AI Empowered helps the reader to consider how local communities may enhance opportunities for entrepreneurship to drive the impact for greater innovation and economic development. This ecosystem of interactions between individuals, industry, colleges and universities, schools and libraries, civil society, and nonprofit and governments may foster the conditions to create economic development and to increase opportunities for employment and entrepreneurship while addressing conditions to improve the persistent barriers to entrepreneurship. It is expected that access to the AI along with positive support for digital literacy and development of skills will lead to individuals achieving important life-changing outcomes. This will depend on the extent to which everyone perceives the relevance of the AI, develops skills for living a part of their life in digital form, and the availability of easy and affordable access to AI platforms, the internet, and devices.

AI Empowered considers the opportunity and challenges for colleges and universities to support entrepreneurship in the AI era. From the perspective of minority serving institutions, AI Empowered takes lessons from historically Black colleges and universities (HBCUs) as part of the local AI ecosystem for entrepreneurship. HBCUs are among the diverse set of stakeholders who serve as community anchor institutions endowed with resources and capabilities to support AI-driven entrepreneurship. This may include access to centers for entrepreneurship, incubator spaces, computer networks and resources, along with the ingenuity of its faculty, students, staff, and alums. The authors help the reader to understand what it takes to align a college or university with other stakeholders in the community to accomplish together what they cannot do separately to support entrepreneurs.

In the closing chapters, AI Empowered helps the reader to name and frame the key challenges for entrepreneurship in the AI era. As generative AI, chatbots and natural language processing, and other uses emerge, the authors shed light on the ethical concerns of AI for responsible innovation. This considers issues with ethical AI development, inclusive data practices, and intellectual property issues that are demonstrated in several case studies. This book primes the reader to participate actively in strategies to help entrepreneurs among African Americans in full consideration of the public policy and ethical context that shapes innovation in the United States and global economy.

Jon Gant, PhD
North Carolina Central University

Preface

> Many times I've felt it's really to our advantage that we don't fit in and that we don't have that seat at that table. That to me is often a benefit because it allows us to step back and really observe in quite an objective way as to where the gaps are and what's needed for change. – Marian Croak, Vice President of Engineering at Google

AI is reshaping our world at an unprecedented pace, transforming industries and redefining opportunities across sectors – from healthcare and education to commerce and community engagement. Yet, as with many technological revolutions, its benefits are not evenly distributed. *AI Empowered: Pioneering African American Entrepreneurship in the Digital Age* investigates how AI intersects with entrepreneurship within the African American community. Rather than focusing on individual biographies or isolated success stories, this book investigates the broader concepts, systemic challenges, and transformative potential that AI holds for African American entrepreneurs and their communities.

The convergence of AI and African American entrepreneurship presents immense possibilities for innovation, growth, and social impact. While AI offers tools that could democratize access to opportunities, significant challenges persist – issues of accessibility, representation, and ethical considerations remain at the forefront. It is vital to take proactive measures to ensure that AI serves as a means of empowerment rather than exacerbating existing disparities. By fostering inclusivity in AI's development and deployment, supporting education and skill development, and addressing structural barriers, we can work toward creating a more equitable entrepreneurial landscape where African American entrepreneurs can thrive and drive meaningful change.

AI holds the promise of an economy where historical barriers such as race, geography, and economic disadvantage no longer determine success. For African American entrepreneurs, this represents a pivotal moment to engage with AI, redefine industries, innovate amid adversity, and build generational wealth. However, these opportunities coexist with significant obstacles rooted in historical inequities, structural disadvantages, and under-representation in the tech industry. This book examines these barriers and envisions pathways to overcome them, laying out a framework for inclusive progress.

Far from being an abstract or inaccessible technology, AI's transformative power lies in its ability to amplify human potential. For African American entrepreneurs, AI can unlock innovation in often-overlooked spaces, transforming community businesses into enterprises with national or global impact. This democratization of technology enables individuals to surmount structural barriers, leveraging AI to turn disparities into opportunities. Yet, realizing this potential requires confronting and addressing systemic biases within technology itself – from algorithmic discrimination to unequal access.

AI Empowered critically examines the frameworks, policies, and practices necessary to ensure that AI fosters equitable progress. It addresses the digital divide, the ethical implications of algorithmic bias, challenges in securing funding, and the importance of education and community networks. Each chapter builds upon the last, offering actionable insights into how African American entrepreneurs can navigate and succeed in the AI-driven economy.

The African American entrepreneurial journey, from the resilience of early Black business pioneers to today's digitally connected startups, is one of creativity, ingenuity, and unwavering determination. By documenting this journey and its intersection with AI, we aim to shift the narrative surrounding technological progress. The African American community, with its history of innovation in the face of adversity, has much to contribute to shaping an equitable AI future. This book serves both as a roadmap for entrepreneurs and a call to action for policymakers, investors, and educators to support these efforts.

Our goal is to illuminate the structural and cultural dimensions of entrepreneurship in the AI era. While we include anonymized case studies and examples inspired by real-world scenarios, they are crafted to illustrate key themes and protect the privacy of the individuals and enterprises involved. This approach keeps the focus on ideas and systemic changes that can empower a new generation of entrepreneurs, rather than on individual narratives.

As you read, we invite you to reflect on AI's transformative potential and its capacity to drive inclusivity and innovation. Whether you are an educator, entrepreneur, technologist, investor, or policymaker, you have a role in ensuring that the AI revolution fosters a more equitable future for all. Let us strive toward a world where technology uplifts communities and bridges divides, enabling everyone to thrive and succeed. This is the promise of AI, not as a tool of exclusion but as a bridge to opportunity and progress.

Introduction

> It's important to be an ally. You don't have to be a Black woman to think we should have more Black women in tech. – Bozoma Saint John, Chief Marketing Officer at Netflix (2020–2022).

The advent of Artificial Intelligence (AI) marks a defining moment in the evolution of entrepreneurship. For African Americans, this technological revolution offers a transformative opportunity to address historical inequities, redefine industries, and create pathways to generational wealth. At its core, this book explores how African American entrepreneurs can harness the power of AI not merely to participate in the global economy but to shape it in meaningful ways. This is not a story about individual success alone; it is an inquiry into the ideas, tools, and systems that can enable inclusive innovation and dismantle systemic barriers.

African American entrepreneurship has long been characterized by resilience and ingenuity – a legacy shaped by both systemic exclusion and creative adaptation. From the self-sustaining enterprises of Reconstruction-era communities to the thriving Black Wall Street of Tulsa, African Americans have built businesses that not only generated economic value but also served as pillars of social and cultural empowerment. These stories of entrepreneurship are a testament to the capacity for innovation, even in the face of adversity. Today, this entrepreneurial spirit is meeting the vast possibilities of AI, a technology capable of amplifying human potential and unlocking new avenues of opportunity.

African American entrepreneurs are innovatively integrating AI across various industries through companies like Gro Intelligence, founded by Sara Menker, which analyzes agricultural data to provide insights on food security and climate change. Silas Adekunle's Reach Industries developed MekaMon, a gaming robot combining augmented reality and AI, and later pivoted to create Lumi, an AI device aiding scientists in data collection and experiment reproducibility. Rodney Williams's Lisnr uses AI to transmit data over audio frequencies for seamless device communication without traditional connectivity. Candace Mitchell-Harris's Myavana offers personalized hair care recommendations by analyzing hair types and conditions with AI. Travis Montaque's Holler enhances digital conversations by suggesting contextually relevant content using AI. Anthony Buchanan's Let Bob AI Momentum ETF simplifies stock market investing with an AI-driven approach, targeting

AI Empowered, 1–8

Published under exclusive licence by Emerald Publishing Limited
doi:10.1108/978-1-83662-816-320251001

underrepresented communities. Skilldora, collaborating with Michael Roberts, provides AI instructor-led courses to students at historically Black colleges and universities (HBCUs). Ellington West's Sonavi Labs develops AI-powered diagnostic tools like smart stethoscopes to improve patient care. Iman Abuzeid's Incredible Health uses AI to efficiently match nurses with hospital job openings. Colin Kaepernick's Lumi Story AI empowers creators with AI tools for content creation, such as generating graphics and pairing illustrations with text. These companies exemplify the innovative application of AI technologies by African American business leaders across diverse fields.

By making use of AI-driven tools, businesses can automate operations, enhance efficiency, and reduce costs, allowing entrepreneurs to focus on strategic growth and customer engagement. For instance, chatbots can handle customer inquiries, while predictive analytics optimize supply chain management, enabling small businesses to compete with larger corporations. AI also provides access to valuable data and insights, helping entrepreneurs analyze market trends, understand customer preferences, and predict opportunities with precision. This data-driven decision-making levels the playing field and fosters innovation. Moreover, AI technologies such as recommendation algorithms and sentiment analysis enable personalized customer engagement, strengthening brand loyalty and creating unique experiences that resonate culturally and emotionally. In terms of education, AI democratizes access to learning through self-paced platforms, mentorship tools, and skill-enhancement programs, addressing systemic gaps and preparing future generations for a tech-driven economy. Finally, AI-powered crowdfunding platforms and fintech solutions offer new pathways to funding, connecting entrepreneurs with aligned investors and providing analytics to refine pitches and improve funding outcomes. Together, these advancements position African American entrepreneurs to thrive in an increasingly AI-dominated world.

It is not an exaggeration to say that AI has shifted the paradigm of entrepreneurship in profound ways. By automating routine tasks, providing advanced data insights, and enabling hyper-personalized customer experiences, AI is reshaping how businesses operate. For African American entrepreneurs, AI can reduce traditional barriers to entry, such as limited access to capital or professional networks, by offering tools that optimize resources and expand reach. Yet, these opportunities come with challenges. Structural inequities, algorithmic biases, and the persistent digital divide threaten to widen disparities if left unchecked. Ensuring that AI serves as a bridge rather than a gatekeeper requires intentionality, education, and advocacy.

Our engagement with thinkers and entrepreneurial practitioners yielded a range of perspectives. The following are some of the quotes we received:

> Artificial Intelligence can be the great equalizer, providing Black entrepreneurs with tools and insights previously inaccessible.

> By harnessing AI, we can bridge the opportunity gap and unlock untapped potential within African American communities.

> AI empowers Black-owned businesses to compete on a global scale by automating processes and enhancing decision-making.

> Through AI-driven mentorship platforms, we can connect emerging Black entrepreneurs with the expertise they need to thrive.
>
> Leveraging AI for market analysis allows African American entrepreneurs to identify and capitalize on niche opportunities.
>
> Artificial Intelligence can help dismantle systemic barriers in funding by providing unbiased credit assessments for Black businesses.
>
> AI can facilitate virtual networks that foster collaboration and innovation among Black entrepreneurs worldwide.
>
> By analyzing cultural trends, AI enables the creation of products and services that resonate deeply with the Black community.
>
> Access to AI education is crucial for empowering the next generation of Black innovators and entrepreneurs.
>
> Embracing AI technology is not just an option but a necessity for Black businesses aiming to lead in the digital economy.

These quotes highlight the range of transformative potential of Artificial Intelligence in empowering African American entrepreneurs.

Sixty-seven entrepreneurs and business executives from African American background completed the survey we shared. Based on feedback to our survey prompts and also based on current thinking as reflected in the literature, the following are some of the central themes related to AI and African American entrepreneurship, according to us.

Transformative Potential of AI in Entrepreneurship

AI is revolutionizing how businesses operate by automating processes, enhancing decision-making, and uncovering new market opportunities. For African American entrepreneurs, AI tools can streamline operations, reduce costs, and enable data-driven strategies. For instance, AI-powered analytics can help identify consumer trends within specific communities, allowing entrepreneurs to tailor products and services effectively.

AI as Both an Enabler and a Disruptor

While AI offers tools that can level the playing field, it also poses risks of widening existing disparities. Accessibility to AI technologies often requires substantial resources, technical expertise, and infrastructure that may not be readily available to all. The digital divide can exacerbate inequalities if not addressed, making AI both a potential catalyst for growth and a barrier to entry.

Accessibility and the Digital Divide

The gap in access to high-speed internet and advanced technologies disproportionately affects African American communities. This digital divide limits the ability of entrepreneurs to utilize AI fully. Efforts to increase access to technology and internet infrastructure are crucial to ensure that the benefits of AI are inclusive.

Cultural and Contextual Relevance in AI Applications

African American entrepreneurs bring unique cultural insights that can inform AI applications, making them more relevant and effective in serving diverse markets. Incorporating cultural nuances into AI algorithms can improve customer engagement and satisfaction in underserved communities.

Representation and Inclusion in AI Development

The lack of diversity in AI development teams can lead to biased algorithms that perpetuate stereotypes and exclude minority perspectives. Increasing representation of African Americans in tech and AI fields is essential to create technologies that are fair and equitable. This includes roles in data science, machine learning, and AI ethics.

Structural Challenges and Barriers

Persistent challenges such as limited access to capital, mentorship, and professional networks hinder the growth of African American entrepreneurship. AI has the potential to mitigate some of these barriers by providing alternative solutions like AI-driven funding platforms or virtual mentorship programs. However, without deliberate efforts to address structural inequities, these tools may not reach those who need them most.

Policy Interventions and Community Initiatives

Government policies and community programs play a pivotal role in bridging gaps. Initiatives that provide funding for tech education, incentives for minority-owned tech startups, and support for incubators can foster an environment where AI is accessible and beneficial to African American entrepreneurs.

Education and Upskilling

Investing in education is crucial to empower entrepreneurs with the skills needed to use AI. This includes promoting STEM education in schools, offering training programs in AI and machine learning, and creating pathways for continuous learning to keep pace with technological advancements. Institutions of higher education play a critical role. HBCUs will be even more central to the upskilling of African Americans in AI.

Ethical Considerations in AI

Ethical issues such as data privacy, algorithmic bias, and transparency are significant concerns. African American entrepreneurs must navigate these challenges to build trust with consumers. Additionally, they have the opportunity to contribute to the development of ethical AI standards that protect minority interests.

Future Outlook and Emerging Opportunities

Looking ahead, AI is expected to become even more integrated into all aspects of business. There is potential for African American entrepreneurs to lead in areas like AI-driven healthcare solutions tailored to minority populations, smart city initiatives in underserved areas, and educational technologies that address learning gaps.

Proactive measures identified in the literature include:

- Collaboration Across Sectors: Partnerships between tech companies, educational institutions (collaboration between K-12 and higher education), and community organizations can facilitate resource sharing and innovation.
- Advocacy for Inclusive AI Policies: Engaging in policy discussions ensures that regulations around AI development and deployment consider the needs of African American entrepreneurs.
- Entrepreneurial Ecosystem Development: Building supportive ecosystems that include access to venture capital, mentorship, and networking opportunities can foster sustainable growth.

Impact on Employment and Economic Opportunities

AI has the potential to create new job categories while rendering some obsolete. Preparing the workforce for this shift is essential. Entrepreneurs can play a role by creating businesses that not only use AI but also contribute to job creation within their communities.

The Role of AI in Social Equity

AI can be a tool for addressing social issues such as healthcare disparities, education gaps, and economic inequality. African American entrepreneurs are uniquely positioned to develop AI solutions that tackle these challenges from an insider's perspective.

This book is about possibilities. Through anonymized case studies and real-world examples, it illustrates how African American entrepreneurs are using AI to transform industries, address community needs, and build scalable enterprises. It exposes the systemic changes needed to create an environment where innovation flourishes equitably, emphasizing the importance of education, mentorship, and inclusive policymaking. The chapters ahead explore these themes in depth. We begin by examining the historical context of African American entrepreneurship and its intersection with technology. From there, we explore the mechanics of AI, the barriers to equitable progress, and the strategies for overcoming those challenges. Each chapter builds toward a vision of the future where African American entrepreneurs are not only participants in the AI revolution but leaders shaping its course. This vision is rooted in the belief that innovation thrives in diversity and that equitable access to technology is essential for sustainable progress.

The core theme of each chapter is summarized below:

Chapter 1: A New Era for African American Entrepreneurship. The entrepreneurial spirit of African Americans, rooted in resilience and cultural identity, is now poised to capitalize AI for unprecedented innovation and economic empowerment.

Chapter 2: The AI Revolution and Its Implications. AI's ability to automate tasks, analyze data, and personalize experiences is reshaping entrepreneurship and creating new pathways for African American businesses to thrive.

Chapter 3: Barriers to Equitable Progress. Addressing systemic inequities and ensuring equitable access to AI technologies are critical to unlocking the full potential of African American entrepreneurship.

Chapter 4: The Digital Divide. Bridging the gap in access to digital tools and AI literacy is essential for enabling African American entrepreneurs to compete in the modern economy.

Chapter 5: Innovation at the Margins. African American entrepreneurs are turning cultural insights into competitive advantages, using AI to create authentic and impactful innovations.

Chapter 6: Policy and Progress. Strategic policy interventions and public–private partnerships can drive equitable AI adoption and support African American entrepreneurial success.

Chapter 7: Funding the Future. AI-driven tools and alternative financing options offer promising solutions to address the funding disparities faced by African American entrepreneurs.

Chapter 8: Education and Empowerment. AI education and STEM initiatives, especially through HBCUs, are vital for empowering the next generation of African American innovators.

Chapter 9: Networking in the AI Era. AI-powered networks and digital mentorship platforms are revolutionizing how African American entrepreneurs connect, collaborate, and innovate globally.

Chapter 10: Global Perspectives on African American Entrepreneurship in AI. Exploring global parallels, African American entrepreneurs can draw inspiration from AI-driven innovations in Africa and the diaspora.

Chapter 11: Ethical AI and Responsible Innovation. Developing inclusive, ethical AI systems is both a moral imperative and a competitive advantage for African American entrepreneurs.

Chapter 12: Leveraging AI for Frugal Innovation. AI-powered frugal innovation is enabling African American entrepreneurs to address underserved markets with cost-effective, high-impact solutions.

Chapter 13: Looking Ahead. The future of African American entrepreneurship lies in embracing AI as a tool for equity, innovation, and leadership in the global economy.

Fig. 1 below is a conceptual mapping of the key ideas presented in this book.

As you embark on this journey, consider your role in this transformative era. Whether you are an entrepreneur, investor, educator, or policymaker, there are opportunities to contribute to a future where AI uplifts all communities. The challenges are significant, but so are the rewards. Let this book inspire you to

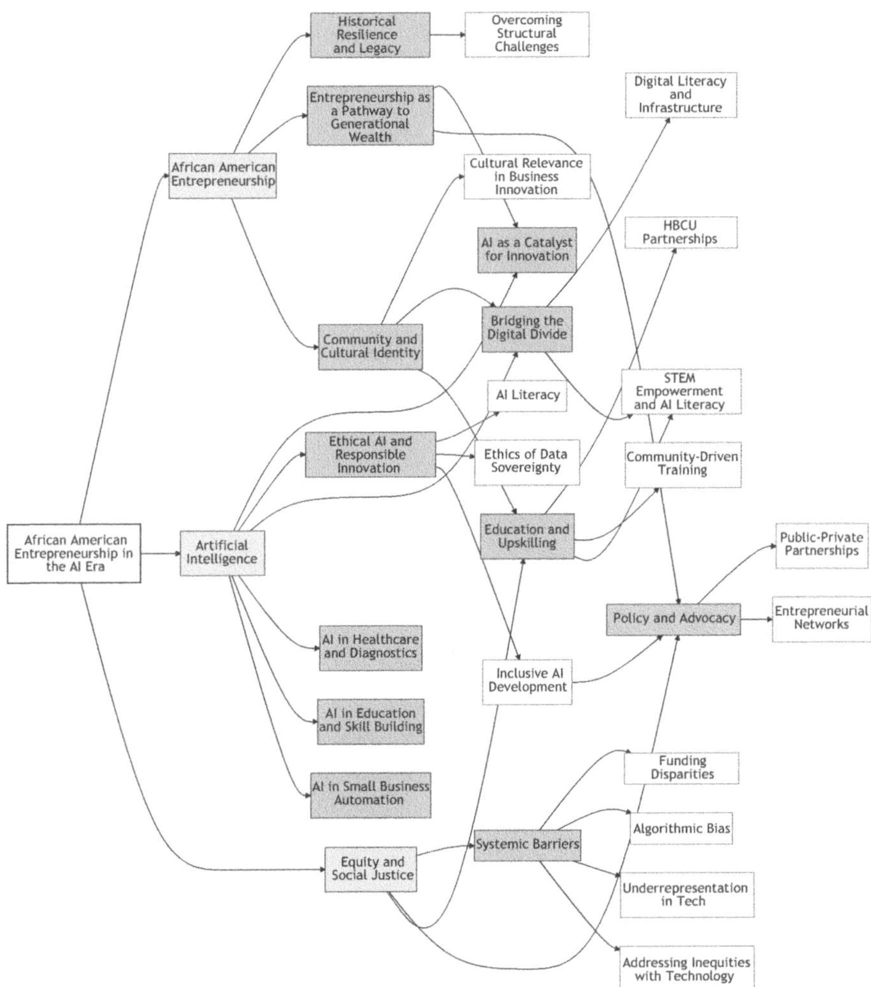

Fig. 1. Key Concepts and Relationships Presented in the Book.

think critically about the potential of AI and to take action toward building an inclusive, equitable digital economy. The future of African American entrepreneurship in the AI age is not predetermined – it is a vision waiting to be realized, and your role in shaping it matters. Together, we can create a world where technology empowers all voices, driving progress and equity for generations to come.

Chapter 1

A New Era for African American Entrepreneurship

> AI is probably the most important thing humanity has ever worked on. I think of it as something more profound than electricity or fire. – Sundar Pichai

The enterprising spirit has long been a cornerstone of the African American community, embodying resilience, ingenuity, and the drive for economic independence. The story of African American entrepreneurship is one of enduring strength against systemic obstacles, innovation in blending culture with commerce, and unified efforts to create opportunities for generational wealth and uplift entire communities. This chapter explores the historical roots of African American entrepreneurship, tracing its growth, influence, and the distinct challenges Black business owners have navigated in the United States.

HeritageYum: Reviving Cultural Businesses Through Technology

Tasha Barber started HeritageYum to celebrate African American culinary traditions in a digital era dominated by algorithmic marketing and personalized experiences. By integrating Artificial Intelligence (AI)-powered recipe customization tools, Tasha was able to transform family-held recipes into adaptive, dynamic dishes that catered to the individual tastes of younger, tech-savvy consumers. AI tools provided deep insights into flavor preferences across different demographics, allowing these restaurants to offer a perfect fusion of tradition and modern tastes, which resonated with the urban millennial. Beyond menu personalization, HeritageYum's AI algorithms also provided marketing insights that strategically targeted culturally receptive audiences across social media, turning these modest family kitchens into celebrated cultural icons. This blend of heritage and technology created a culinary renaissance that not only honored African American roots but also equipped small business owners with tools to thrive globally in the digital economy.

AI Empowered, 9–15

Published under exclusive licence by Emerald Publishing Limited
doi:10.1108/978-1-83662-816-320251002

A Legacy of Resilience and Innovation

The history of African American entrepreneurship is deeply intertwined with the struggle for equality and self-determination. From the earliest days of Reconstruction, when freed slaves sought to build their own economic futures, to the modern era of technological advancement, Black entrepreneurs have consistently demonstrated a remarkable ability to overcome adversity and create opportunities.

Following emancipation, many African Americans embarked on a journey to establish themselves economically despite the lingering constraints of systemic discrimination. During Reconstruction, newly freed African Americans built enterprises not only to sustain themselves but also to support and uplift their communities, a hallmark of the African American Tradition. Early Black-owned businesses were often modest but vital in scale, serving as community hubs that provided essential goods and services. These enterprises fostered a sense of collective self-reliance, where businesses not only met local needs but also played significant roles in social and political activism – challenging segregation, promoting education, and advocating for civil rights.

Many of these early ventures faced immense challenges, including hostile local environments, discriminatory laws, violence, and a lack of access to financial capital. Despite these barriers, Black entrepreneurs laid the foundation for economic independence that became a pillar of the community. It was not only about profit – these businesses represented freedom, dignity, and a means of creating stability in a society that actively sought to deny such opportunities to African Americans. Entrepreneurs like Henry Boyd, who invented a unique type of bedstead, and the countless unnamed individuals who set up laundries, grocery stores, and barber shops, were pioneers of resilience. They showed that even in a nation marred by segregation, African Americans could chart their own course toward empowerment.

Entrepreneurship as a Vehicle for Social Mobility

For African Americans, entrepreneurship has long been a vital pathway to social mobility, offering opportunities for economic independence and generational wealth. The businesses founded during Reconstruction, such as barbershops, grocery stores, and newspapers, were far more than commercial ventures; they symbolized self-determination and resilience in the face of systemic oppression. These establishments provided safe spaces for networking, education, and political organizing, strengthening the social fabric of Black communities and laying the groundwork for future generations to thrive.

Even during periods of segregation, Black-owned businesses carved out spheres where African Americans could thrive in an otherwise discriminatory society. Barber shops and beauty salons, for example, were not only profitable ventures but also cultural centers where people could gather, share ideas, and support one another. Today, entrepreneurship continues to serve as a catalyst for economic empowerment. African American business owners use digital platforms and AI to overcome new challenges, charting innovative courses toward greater autonomy and opportunity. Businesses like The Honey Pot, founded by Beatrice Dixon, and Blavity, created by Morgan DeBaun, are prime examples of how the entrepreneurial spirit endures and evolves, embracing technology to reach new heights.

The intergenerational impact of entrepreneurship is significant. Families who own and operate businesses often have opportunities to build wealth that extends beyond mere profit margins. Children who grow up in entrepreneurial households frequently gain firsthand experience in managing finances, strategizing for growth, and engaging in problem-solving. This exposure provides invaluable life lessons and skills that help to break cycles of poverty and dependency. In Black communities, where systemic inequities have made traditional wealth-building avenues difficult to access, entrepreneurship stands as a powerful alternative route for creating financial stability and generational success.

Cultural Identity as a Source of Innovation

African American entrepreneurs have historically drawn strength from their cultural identity, using it as a unique source of innovation and differentiation. Madam C.J. Walker, often cited as the first self-made female millionaire in the United States, developed beauty products specifically tailored to the needs of Black women, establishing an industry that celebrated and empowered African American beauty. Fast forward to the late 20th century, and a figure like Jay-Z, who used the influence of hip-hop culture to build global brands that transformed music, fashion, and business.

The influence of cultural identity extends beyond individual products to the establishment of broader cultural narratives. These entrepreneurs have consistently demonstrated how deeply rooted cultural experiences can translate into successful ventures. Today, cultural identity remains a powerful driving force for African American entrepreneurship. In the age of artificial intelligence, entrepreneurs are creating technologies that reflect and address the unique experiences of Black communities. From developing algorithms that counter cultural biases in healthcare to creating media platforms that amplify underrepresented voices, African American business owners are proving that cultural authenticity can intersect with technological innovation to produce both social impact and business success.

The use of culture as an asset also helps to create authentic and compelling brand identities that resonate deeply with consumers. Cultural pride, heritage, and shared experiences create a connection between Black-owned businesses and their customers. This authenticity is something that cannot be easily replicated by competitors who lack the lived experiences that are foundational to these brands. The richness of African American culture has been, and continues to be, a powerful tool for both economic success and cultural influence.

Intersectionality: The Double Bind of Race and Technology

African American entrepreneurs face unique barriers at the intersection of race and technology. The challenges posed by racial inequities are compounded by the rapid pace of technological change, requiring extraordinary resilience and ingenuity to overcome. Historically, Black business owners were systematically excluded from capital markets and lucrative industries, often forced to carve out niches in community-based businesses and sectors where they could sustain themselves without external support.

In today's AI-driven economy, similar challenges persist. Access to high-quality STEM education, industry networks, and venture capital remains disproportionately limited for African Americans, creating significant obstacles for aspiring tech entrepreneurs. The digital divide continues to exacerbate existing inequalities, where gaps in access to education and technology lead to fewer opportunities for African American entrepreneurs to participate in the emerging tech economy.

Targeted interventions are essential to bridge these gaps. Collaborations with historically Black colleges and universities (HBCUs), for example, can play a critical role in ensuring that African American students gain access to AI education, training, and the opportunities necessary to thrive in the tech industry. Initiatives like coding boot camps and tech incubators specifically aimed at underrepresented groups are also key in leveling the playing field. The efforts to bridge the gap must also involve public–private partnerships that commit to providing resources, mentorship, and funding to aspiring Black tech entrepreneurs.

Cultural Impact and Branding

African American entrepreneurship has always been closely linked to cultural expression. From the vibrant jazz clubs of the Harlem Renaissance to the influential hip-hop labels of the 1990s, Black-owned businesses have served as spaces for cultural production, community gathering, and social change. These businesses have not only shaped African American cultural identity but also had a lasting impact on broader American society, influencing music, fashion, language, and social movements.

Branding, too, has played a crucial role in the success of African American enterprises. Many Black entrepreneurs have drawn upon their cultural heritage to create distinctive brands that resonate deeply with consumers. Companies like FUBU and Rocawear leveraged the global appeal of hip-hop culture to connect with audiences that valued authenticity and identity, turning cultural affinity into economic success. This ability to link cultural identity with business branding has enabled African American entrepreneurs to build brands that are not only profitable but also socially meaningful.

The cultural impact of these businesses is profound. They do more than sell products – they tell stories, evoke emotions, and offer representation in industries where African Americans have historically been marginalized. The success of

Black-owned brands highlights the intersection between cultural pride and economic achievement. Brands like Pyer Moss by Kerby Jean-Raymond and Mielle Organics by Monique Rodriguez continue this tradition of infusing culture into business, demonstrating that when a brand authentically represents its community, it resonates on a profound level.

The Power of Community Entrepreneurship

African American entrepreneurship has often thrived within a collective, community-driven framework. One of the most powerful examples of this communal spirit was the Greenwood District of Tulsa, Oklahoma, also known as "Black Wall Street." In Greenwood, African American entrepreneurs created a thriving economic ecosystem, reinvesting profits into the local community and fostering shared prosperity. Businesses in the Greenwood District spanned industries from retail and hospitality to banking, serving as a testament to what was possible when Black communities worked together to overcome systemic barriers.

Today, digital platforms offer new possibilities for this kind of community-focused entrepreneurship. Crowdfunding, online cooperatives, and AI-powered marketplaces enable African American entrepreneurs to build interconnected networks that can support shared growth and resilience. Revisiting the historical model of collective economic empowerment in a modern context provides valuable insights for creating inclusive and sustainable entrepreneurial ecosystems. Platforms like Black and Mobile, which exclusively partners with Black-owned restaurants, show how technology can be harnessed to foster economic growth within the community.

Community-driven entrepreneurship extends beyond profit – it is about nurturing environments where Black entrepreneurs can access resources, collaborate, and innovate. By focusing on community wealth-building, African American entrepreneurs can create ecosystems that are more resilient to economic downturns and shifts in the broader market. The sense of shared destiny that characterized initiatives like Black Wall Street is being reimagined in today's world through digital tools and online collaboration, setting the stage for a new era of collective economic empowerment.

Overcoming Barriers

The journey of African American entrepreneurship has been characterized by resilience in the face of persistent barriers. Systemic challenges such as limited access to capital, racial discrimination, and underrepresentation in certain industries have created significant obstacles for Black entrepreneurs. Despite these difficulties, many African Americans have found ways to navigate these barriers through innovation, determination, and community support.

Building strong networks, leveraging community resources, and seeking mentorship from successful entrepreneurs are some of the strategies that have helped Black business owners overcome these obstacles. Crowd funding and alternative financing options have also been crucial in addressing the challenges of limited access to traditional capital markets, allowing entrepreneurs to generate the funds needed to launch and scale their businesses. Organizations such as the National Black MBA Association and the Minority Business Development Agency play important roles in connecting Black entrepreneurs with resources and support.

The role of financial literacy in overcoming these barriers is also paramount. Many Black entrepreneurs face challenges due to a lack of exposure to financial management tools and knowledge. Programs that focus on financial literacy, paired with access to capital, can help empower aspiring business owners. By understanding how to manage cash flow, secure loans, and attract investors, African American entrepreneurs can better position themselves to succeed in an often-unforgiving business landscape.

Community and Education: Foundations for Success

The role of community in nurturing African American entrepreneurship is immense. Support networks, including mentorship programs and entrepreneurial communities, provide essential guidance, knowledge, and opportunities for collaboration. These networks are vital in offering access to capital and in helping entrepreneurs navigate the complex landscape of business ownership. Peer mentoring and mutual support have long been critical components of Black entrepreneurship, providing emotional support and practical advice.

Education also plays a pivotal role in empowering African American entrepreneurs. HBCUs have been instrumental in providing access to higher education and specialized training, helping to foster an entrepreneurial mindset within Black communities. Additionally, community education programs and online learning platforms have become valuable resources for acquiring the skills necessary to succeed in today's digital economy. Ensuring equitable access to quality education and training remains a key factor in leveling the playing field for African American entrepreneurs.

The importance of STEM education cannot be ignored, especially as technology becomes increasingly integrated into all sectors of business. Programs that introduce African American youth to coding, robotics, and AI can help build a pipeline of future entrepreneurs equipped with the skills needed to thrive in a tech-driven economy. Community organizations like Black Girls CODE are providing invaluable services by preparing the next generation of Black tech entrepreneurs, emphasizing both technical and entrepreneurial skills.

The Path Forward: Innovation and Opportunity

The historical journey of African American entrepreneurship provides valuable lessons for future generations. Resilience, community support, and innovation have been essential for overcoming challenges and achieving success. To foster a robust entrepreneurial ecosystem for the future, it is vital to invest in education, address systemic barriers to capital, establish mentorship programs, and advocate for policies that support minority-owned businesses.

The dawn of artificial intelligence marks a pivotal moment for African American entrepreneurs. Just as the industrial revolution redefined economic landscapes, AI offers tools that have the potential to dismantle traditional barriers and democratize innovation. Affordable cloud-based AI solutions, global digital marketplaces, and advanced data analytics are now accessible, allowing entrepreneurs to make informed decisions and scale their businesses in ways previously unimaginable.

However, the opportunities presented by AI come with unique risks, such as algorithmic bias and unequal access to technological resources. African American entrepreneurs are uniquely positioned to lead efforts in addressing these challenges, advocating for fairness and inclusion, and developing AI-driven solutions tailored to marginalized communities. By leveraging their cultural identity, community networks, and resilience, African American business owners can not only advance their own economic futures but also contribute meaningfully to creating a more equitable society.

To truly build a future where African American entrepreneurship thrives, concerted efforts from both public and private sectors are necessary. This includes creating funding opportunities specifically aimed at Black entrepreneurs, supporting initiatives that promote diversity in the tech industry, and encouraging the creation of more inclusive educational curriculums. By addressing these issues head-on, society can ensure that African American entrepreneurs are given the tools they need to succeed, contributing to a more dynamic and equitable economy. The path forward is clear: innovation, community, and cultural pride will continue to be the bedrock of African American entrepreneurial success.

Inspiration Bite: Nashlie Sephus

Dr. Nashlie Sephus is the Principal AI/ML Evangelist for Amazon AI, focusing on fairness and identifying biases in AWS AI technologies. She formerly led the Amazon Visual Search team in Atlanta, which launched visual search for replacement parts on the Amazon Shopping app in June 2018. This technology was a result of her former startup, Partpic, being acquired by Amazon, where she served as the Chief Technology Officer. Beyond her corporate role, Dr. Sephus is the founder and CEO of The Bean Path, a nonprofit organization based in Jackson, Mississippi, dedicated to providing technical expertise and guidance to individuals and small businesses, thereby fostering technological growth and innovation in her community.

Source: https://www.beanpath.org/team/dr.-nashlie-sephus

Reflection Prompts

How can the legacy of African American entrepreneurial resilience inspire you to innovate in your own ventures?

In what ways can you weave cultural identity into your business model to create both social and economic impact?

What steps can you take today to ensure that your entrepreneurial efforts contribute to generational wealth and uplift the African American community?

Chapter 2

The AI Revolution and Its Implications

> We do not believe that AI is going to [cause] an employment apocalypse. Although it is true that millions of jobs are going to be lost and millions of jobs are going to be created, the augmentation side is the transformation side. – Gilbert Fossoun Houngbo, Director-General of the International Labour Organization.

Artificial Intelligence (AI) is rapidly transforming our world, revolutionizing industries, and fundamentally reshaping the ways we live and work. This chapter investigates deeply into the core concepts of AI, tracing its evolution through different waves, and examining its profound impact on entrepreneurship. By focusing on how AI empowers entrepreneurs – particularly those from historically marginalized communities – we reveal how technology is breaking down barriers, enabling innovative solutions, and driving progress in tackling real-world challenges. We explore the promise, the opportunities, and the potential pitfalls of AI, ensuring a comprehensive understanding of its current role and its future trajectory.

EducateArtificialIntelligence: Tailoring Education for Underserved Students

The founder of EducateArtificialIntelligence was a visionary who understood that AI could bridge the educational divide faced by students in underfunded school districts. They launched EducateArtificialIntelligence with the goal of transforming STEM education by customizing the learning experience for each student, no matter their starting point. By analyzing intricate data on students' learning habits, gaps in understanding, and engagement levels, EducateArtificialIntelligence crafted personalized learning paths that addressed each student's unique needs. This AI-driven platform didn't just stop at identifying gaps; it became a virtual mentor that adjusted lesson plans in real time, empowering teachers with the insights to be more effective in their classrooms. In doing so, Amara's initiative created an inclusive learning ecosystem where

AI Empowered, 17–25

Published under exclusive licence by Emerald Publishing Limited
doi:10.1108/978-1-83662-816-320251003

underserved students could gain a competitive edge, turning educational barriers into springboards toward STEM careers and future opportunities in the AI economy.

Understanding AI: Beyond the Buzzword

AI is more than just a trending buzzword; it signifies a fundamental shift in how humans interact with machines and data, affecting almost every aspect of our daily lives and business practices. At its core, AI involves the development of computer systems capable of performing tasks that traditionally require human intelligence, such as learning, reasoning, problem-solving, and understanding language. Far from being a static concept, AI has undergone a complex and dynamic evolutionary journey, marked by key milestones that have shaped its current capabilities and propelled it into mainstream consciousness.

The first wave of AI innovation, spanning from the 1950s to the 1980s, saw the creation of early computer programs that could perform simple tasks such as playing games, solving algebraic equations, and speaking rudimentary English. These foundational breakthroughs laid the groundwork for future developments, sparking curiosity and excitement about the possibilities of machines that could mimic human thought processes. However, these early systems were limited by the computational power of the time, which restricted their real-world applicability.

The second wave of AI innovation, between the 1980s and 2010, introduced machine learning – a concept where computers could learn from data without requiring explicit instructions. This advancement enabled the rise of neural networks, which facilitated powerful capabilities in pattern recognition, data processing, and prediction. During this period, AI began transitioning from a research-focused field into practical applications that added value across different industries. Machine learning's success in analyzing data, recognizing patterns, and making predictions opened up new possibilities, providing a glimpse of the immense potential AI held for transforming businesses.

The third and current wave, beginning around 2010, is characterized by deep learning – a leap forward that allows neural networks to learn from vast datasets, mimicking the human brain's processing patterns in complex ways. This era has fueled major breakthroughs in areas such as image recognition, natural language processing, autonomous systems, and numerous sophisticated applications that are now transforming both daily life and the way businesses operate. This modern wave of AI is powered by the availability of big data, advances in computing power, and improvements in algorithms, leading to a surge of innovations that we see today. From self-driving cars to virtual assistants, deep learning has positioned AI as a force that is shaping the future in unprecedented ways.

AI and Entrepreneurship: A New Paradigm

AI is not just a technological development; it is reshaping the startup ecosystem by providing powerful tools that empower entrepreneurs to innovate, optimize, and scale effectively. For many startups, particularly those led by historically underrepresented communities, AI offers a pathway to overcome longstanding obstacles and access new avenues for success. This technology is democratizing opportunities by leveling the playing field for those who have traditionally faced systemic barriers, allowing them to compete on a global scale.

One of AI's most significant contributions to entrepreneurship is automation. Entrepreneurs can now automate repetitive and mundane tasks, freeing up time to focus on strategic decision-making, creative pursuits, and business growth. This capability allows smaller enterprises, which may lack resources, to achieve efficiencies that were previously only possible for larger companies. By streamlining operations, AI enables businesses to prioritize the kind of high-level thinking that drives innovation and fuels growth. Additionally, AI's sophisticated data analysis capabilities allow entrepreneurs to derive valuable insights from large volumes of information, including customer behavior, market trends, and operational performance. These insights empower businesses to make informed, data-driven decisions that enhance their competitive edge and long-term viability.

AI has also revolutionized the customer experience, enabling personalized and immediate interactions that build loyalty and enhance satisfaction. AI-driven chatbots, recommendation systems, and virtual assistants deliver tailored, round-the-clock support, which is particularly beneficial for startups with limited resources. Such capabilities allow businesses to offer seamless customer service experiences that not only meet but exceed customer expectations. By optimizing business processes and improving overall efficiency, AI ultimately helps startups reduce operational costs, improve product quality, and boost profitability. Thus, AI isn't just a technical tool; it is a fundamental enabler that redefines how entrepreneurs start, grow, and sustain their ventures.

Beyond automation and efficiency, AI provides a powerful suite of tools for fostering innovation. Tools like Chatfuel and MobileMonkey help entrepreneurs automate customer service, while marketing automation platforms such as HubSpot streamline email campaigns, social media postings, and lead generation. Sales forecasting tools, like those offered by Salesforce, harness AI to deliver data-driven insights into market trends, while platforms such as Tableau help interpret complex data into actionable business strategies. Collectively, these AI-driven solutions empower entrepreneurs to navigate the complexities of the digital economy with agility, allowing them to identify opportunities and address challenges in real-time. The use of AI gives businesses a crucial competitive edge in a rapidly evolving marketplace, enabling them to adapt to changes and capitalize on emerging trends.

Data: The New Currency of the Digital Age

In today's digital landscape, data has emerged as one of the most valuable assets for businesses, often referred to as the "new currency" of the digital age. This vast collection of information has the potential to serve numerous strategic purposes, fueling business growth, innovation, and personalized customer experiences. By leveraging predictive analytics, businesses can anticipate future trends and behaviors, allowing them to stay ahead of market shifts and respond proactively to changing conditions. This anticipatory power enables businesses to tailor products, services, and marketing strategies to meet emerging customer demands and maximize their market presence.

Data's value extends to operational efficiency as well. By identifying bottlenecks and areas for improvement, big data helps businesses optimize their processes, minimize waste, and boost productivity. For instance, data analytics can reveal inefficiencies in supply chains, allowing companies to reconfigure their logistics and maximize throughput. Furthermore, big data plays a critical role in risk management by enabling companies to predict potential risks and take proactive measures to mitigate them. These predictive capabilities are essential for enhancing overall financial stability, making businesses more resilient in the face of uncertainty and disruption.

However, the immense power of data brings forth significant ethical considerations. The responsible use of data involves ensuring robust data protection measures, adhering to privacy laws such as the General Data Protection Regulation (GDPR) and California Consumer Privacy Act (CCPA), and upholding ethical standards that prevent discrimination and misuse. Transparency is vital – businesses must be clear about how they collect, use, and store customer data to foster trust. Customers want to know that their data is secure and being used for purposes they understand and approve of. While data is indeed a powerful asset, its use must be carefully balanced with respect for individual privacy and a commitment to ethical practices to avoid potential backlash and ensure sustainable growth.

Success Stories: AI Entrepreneurship in Action

The year 2023 saw a significant surge in the development and adoption of generative AI, with advanced models beginning to rival and even surpass human capabilities in complex tasks. Despite ongoing concerns regarding transparency, bias, and ethical dilemmas, many entrepreneurs have harnessed AI's potential to drive impactful change. Creative tech minds have utilized AI to create innovative solutions across a range of sectors, including agriculture, education, and healthcare. These success stories illustrate AI's transformative power to empower individuals, reshape industries, and open up new possibilities for growth and advancement.

For instance, Sara Menker's work in agricultural data has helped address critical challenges in food security, offering data-driven insights that improve agricultural productivity. Kimberly Bryant, through Black Girls CODE, has made use of AI to inspire and educate the next generation of young women of color, providing them with the tools and knowledge needed to thrive in the tech industry. Ilarna Nche has used AI to develop creative and impactful applications to make a range of consumer-focused services more accessible. These entrepreneurs demonstrate how AI can be a force for good, creating opportunities that drive both economic and social progress.

AI Beyond Automation: Redefining Creativity and Innovation

Although much of the conversation around AI centers on automation, its potential to augment human creativity is equally transformative. For African American entrepreneurs, AI offers unparalleled opportunities to create culturally resonant content by analyzing societal trends, historical data, and user preferences. Generative AI platforms support creative pursuits in design, storytelling, music composition, and film production, democratizing access to industries that have traditionally required substantial resources. This democratization allows African American entrepreneurs to challenge stereotypes, redefine cultural narratives, and produce content that resonates globally, enhancing representation and inclusion in the digital space.

Generative AI tools, such as those used in visual design and video production, enable creators to produce high-quality work without the need for expensive equipment or extensive technical expertise. AI-powered platforms can analyze user preferences, making it easier for creators to produce content that appeals to diverse audiences, thus broadening their reach and impact. By leveraging AI, African American entrepreneurs can address underrepresentation in media and entertainment by creating authentic content that tells their stories and highlights their experiences. This type of content not only entertains but also educates, inspiring meaningful dialogue and bridging cultural gaps.

Ethical AI: Challenges and Opportunities

The rapid adoption of AI has raised urgent ethical questions, particularly around bias, inclusivity, and accountability. African American entrepreneurs have a unique opportunity to lead in the development of ethical AI systems that prioritize fairness and inclusivity. This leadership can involve advocating for diverse datasets that better represent marginalized communities, developing tools that identify and mitigate bias in existing AI systems, and promoting transparency in AI decision-making processes. By ensuring that AI systems are built with inclusivity in mind, African American entrepreneurs can help prevent the perpetuation of biases that have historically disadvantaged their communities.

The ethical AI movement aligns with broader values of equity and justice, giving African American entrepreneurs a platform to influence the future direction of AI policy and practice. Moreover, by participating in the creation of ethical AI standards, these entrepreneurs can help establish best practices that ensure AI technologies are used responsibly. This includes advocating for policies that promote diversity in AI research, supporting initiatives aimed at increasing AI literacy within underrepresented communities, and collaborating with stakeholders to create inclusive technological frameworks. Ethical AI is not only a moral imperative but also a competitive advantage, as consumers increasingly demand technologies that align with their values.

Data Sovereignty: Ownership in the Digital Era

In an AI-driven economy, data is not only a resource but also a source of power and influence. For African American entrepreneurs, issues of data sovereignty are particularly crucial. It is essential that ownership of data sourced from Black communities benefits those communities, rather than being exploited by external entities for profit without any return. Respecting data privacy and ethical standards ensures that community-generated data is used responsibly to address the specific needs of the community, creating value that flows back to the people who provide it.

By establishing frameworks for data ownership, African American entrepreneurs can position themselves as leaders in building trustworthy AI ecosystems that prioritize fairness, transparency, and community well-being. This includes creating data-driven platforms that directly benefit Black communities, using data insights to address issues like access to education, healthcare disparities, and economic inequities. Data sovereignty empowers communities by giving them control over how their data is collected, analyzed, and utilized, ensuring that technological progress is inclusive and equitable.

Collaborative Ecosystems: Building AI Partnerships

AI development thrives in collaborative environments, where knowledge-sharing and partnership can accelerate innovation. For African American entrepreneurs, forming partnerships is a powerful way to broaden access to resources and drive impactful AI solutions. Collaborations with historically Black colleges and universities (HBCUs) and research institutions can foster AI research tailored to the unique needs of Black communities, ensuring that solutions are relevant and impactful. Such collaborations can also help bridge the gap between academic research and real-world application, translating theoretical AI concepts into practical tools that create tangible value.

Partnering with established tech giants can provide access to advanced AI tools, mentorship, and networks that open doors to global markets. These partnerships can serve as a critical resource for startups that may lack the infrastructure to scale independently. Additionally, grassroots coalitions can pool resources, share expertise, and develop community-driven solutions that address local challenges. These collaborative efforts help bridge the resource gap, enabling African American entrepreneurs to compete on a larger scale, amplify their impact, and foster a culture of innovation within their communities.

AI for Social Good: Addressing Community-Specific Issues

AI's potential for social impact is immense, particularly when used to address issues that affect underserved communities. African American entrepreneurs are uniquely positioned to figure out AI for social good, using technology to tackle challenges that disproportionately impact their communities. In healthcare, for instance, AI can help develop predictive models for early detection of conditions like diabetes, hypertension, and other illnesses that disproportionately affect African American populations. These models can improve healthcare access and outcomes, ultimately saving lives and reducing disparities in health services.

In education, AI-driven personalized learning platforms can help close achievement gaps in underserved schools by catering to diverse learning styles and providing students with tailored resources that address their unique needs. These platforms can foster a more inclusive educational environment, enabling students who may have struggled in traditional settings to thrive. In the criminal justice system, AI tools can analyze biases in sentencing and policing, providing insights that support reform efforts and promote transparency. Such applications of AI not only drive business success but also foster meaningful societal change, making AI a tool for empowerment and progress.

AI and Entrepreneurship Training

To fully harness the potential of AI, entrepreneurs need more than just technical knowledge – they require entrepreneurial insight, business acumen, and an understanding of how to integrate AI into their business strategies. Training programs that focus on integrating AI into business models, validating market demand through AI tools, and developing funding strategies tailored for AI ventures are crucial for success. Such programs should emphasize actionable knowledge, empowering entrepreneurs to translate AI concepts into scalable businesses and to navigate the complexities of an AI-driven economy.

Effective training should also include aspects of AI ethics, responsible data use, and understanding the societal implications of AI adoption. By providing entrepreneurs with a well-rounded education that addresses both technical and ethical components, training programs can ensure that businesses are built on a foundation of responsibility, fairness, and inclusivity. Entrepreneurs need to understand not only how AI can improve efficiency and profitability but also how it can be used to create positive social impact, thereby building a business that is both successful and conscientious.

AI and the Future of Work for Entrepreneurs

AI is reshaping the labor market, creating opportunities for entrepreneurs to reimagine the future of work and redefine the employer–employee relationship. African American entrepreneurs can seize these opportunities by developing AI-driven platforms that cater to niche markets within the gig economy. AI also facilitates the creation of tools that support remote work, enhancing productivity, communication, and collaboration. Remote work platforms powered by AI can optimize task assignments, track progress, and provide insights into team productivity, ensuring that businesses can operate effectively even in distributed environments.

Furthermore, AI-powered reskilling platforms can prepare workers for the AI economy, addressing unemployment and skill gaps in communities that are often left behind by technological advancements. By creating AI-driven learning experiences, these platforms can provide personalized training paths that help workers develop the skills needed for emerging job roles. For entrepreneurs, understanding and leveraging these trends provides a unique opportunity to build businesses that not only anticipate the future of work but also create meaningful opportunities for individuals within their communities, driving economic growth and social empowerment.

Navigating the AI Landscape: Challenges and Opportunities

Navigating the AI landscape involves both opportunities and challenges. Entrepreneurs must grapple with regulatory complexities, talent acquisition, integrating new technologies within existing systems, and addressing ethical concerns. Overcoming these hurdles requires strategic planning, adaptability, and a willingness to learn continuously. Although there are fears of AI-induced unemployment, the technology also has the potential to create new jobs by automating repetitive tasks and stimulating economic growth. Preparing the workforce for an AI-driven future involves investing in training, reskilling, and creating supportive economic policies that foster innovation while ensuring inclusivity.

Incorporating the AI revolution requires recognizing it as a general-purpose technology that impacts nearly every industry. Continuous learning and adaptability are essential for entrepreneurs seeking to harness AI's full potential and thrive in an ever-evolving technological landscape. By understanding and effectively utilizing AI, entrepreneurs can build a future where innovation and inclusivity go hand in hand. The journey involves not only leveraging AI to drive business success but also ensuring that the benefits of technological advancement are shared equitably, contributing to a more just and prosperous society for all.

Inspiration Bite: Timnit Gebru

Dr. Timnit Gebru is a prominent computer scientist specializing in algorithmic bias and data mining. She co-founded Black in AI, an advocacy group promoting the inclusion of Black individuals in artificial intelligence research and development. Dr. Gebru's work has been instrumental in highlighting the ethical implications of AI technologies, particularly concerning large language models. In December 2020, she was controversially terminated from her role as co-lead of Google's Ethical AI team after raising concerns about bias in AI systems. Following her departure, she founded the Distributed Artificial Intelligence Research Institute (DAIR), focusing on independent, community-rooted AI research free from Big Tech's influence.

Source: https://www.historyofdatascience.com/timnit-gebru-the-computer-scientist-fighting-for-a-fairer-world/

Reflection Prompts

How comfortable are you with AI technologies? What steps can you take to better understand or use them?

What areas of your life or business could be transformed by automating tasks with AI?

What potential do you see for AI to solve problems in the African American community?

Chapter 3

Barriers to Equitable Progress

> Injustice anywhere is a threat to justice everywhere. – Martin Luther King Jr.

The transformative potential of Artificial Intelligence (AI) is undeniable, yet its benefits are at risk of being unevenly distributed if historical inequities and systemic barriers remain unaddressed. This chapter explores the complex challenges faced by African American entrepreneurs in the AI space, examining the digital divide and the obstacles that hinder their participation in this technological revolution. By highlighting both the difficulties and potential pathways to a more inclusive future, we aim to emphasize the urgency of equitable progress and the hope for transformative change. The central question is how we can create an AI landscape that truly benefits everyone, regardless of race or background, and how we can empower African American entrepreneurs to thrive in this new economy.

AI Healthcare Company: Fighting Healthcare Inequities With Data

AI Healthcare Company emerged as a critical tool in reducing chronic health disparities affecting African American communities. By leveraging AI and machine learning, AI Healthcare Company's platform analyzed social determinants of health, community-specific behavioral data, and genetic predispositions to predict trends in chronic illnesses. This foresight enabled community clinics to proactively design intervention programs, improve patient engagement, and allocate resources where they were most needed. Even in the face of funding inequities, AI Healthcare Company successfully secured a partnership with a government agency by demonstrating the substantial societal impact of his platform – using AI not only to predict health trends but also to advocate for policy changes and funding reallocations. AI Healthcare Company redefined healthcare for marginalized communities, proving that data-driven insights could not only save lives but also reshape public health strategies to be more inclusive and equitable.

AI Empowered, 27–35

doi:10.1108/978-1-83662-816-320251004

The Legacy of Exclusion in Business

The legacy of systemic exclusion has left a persistent gap in opportunities for African American entrepreneurs. For generations, practices such as redlining denied Black communities access to essential financial resources, while discriminatory education and hiring systems further exacerbated barriers to economic advancement. These historical injustices continue to reverberate, as African Americans are underrepresented in STEM fields and often struggle with limited access to venture capital. The systemic exclusion not only affected financial access but also perpetuated a social stigma that kept African American communities from benefiting from wealth-building opportunities that could help uplift entire generations.

These barriers are not simply remnants of the past – they are actively perpetuated by modern technologies, often in ways that are less visible but equally damaging. For example, algorithms trained on biased data can reinforce existing disparities. AI tools used in hiring may unintentionally exclude talented individuals from Black communities, compounding the existing challenges. Addressing these inequities requires more than acknowledging historical injustices; it requires a concerted effort to reshape technology and society to be fairer and more inclusive. This reshaping involves deliberate interventions to ensure that AI systems do not encode or amplify the biases of the past but instead provide equitable opportunities for all.

The entrepreneurial journey for African Americans has always been defined by resilience and ingenuity, often in the face of institutional adversity. From the postslavery era to the Jim Crow years and beyond, discriminatory policies such as Black Codes and redlining limited access to credit and market opportunities. The exclusion from mainstream banking institutions forced many African Americans to rely on informal networks for capital, which, while supportive, lacked the scale needed for significant economic growth. Despite these barriers, African Americans have demonstrated an enduring spirit of entrepreneurship, creating thriving businesses that serve their communities and extend well beyond. This resilience is evident in the numerous success stories of Black-owned businesses that not only survived but flourished, building community wealth and providing essential services.

Systemic Challenges and Their Impact on Entrepreneurship

Systemic challenges continue to overshadow the aspirations of African American entrepreneurs today, manifesting in multiple forms. The lack of access to startup capital remains a significant hurdle, often driven by biases in lending practices and exclusion from venture capital networks. African American entrepreneurs frequently face discriminatory lending standards, which restrict their ability to secure the funding necessary to grow their businesses. This creates a cycle of underfunding that prevents businesses from reaching their full potential.

Underrepresentation in technology and innovation is rooted in educational disparities, with unequal access to quality schooling and limited early exposure to

STEM subjects acting as significant obstacles. The digital divide is exacerbated by the lack of representation of African American teachers and mentors in STEM disciplines, further discouraging young students from pursuing these fields. Furthermore, exclusion from professional networks restricts vital business connections, limiting access to mentorship and collaborative opportunities that are often crucial for success. Many African American entrepreneurs also lack access to the informal networks that are often vital for gaining entry to funding opportunities and strategic partnerships.

These obstacles are compounded by disproportionate scrutiny and higher performance expectations placed on African American entrepreneurs compared to their counterparts. Investors and stakeholders often demand higher proof of concept and scalability from Black business owners, creating additional pressures that are not as commonly faced by others. Even so, African American business owners have consistently shown remarkable resilience, contributing meaningfully to the digital economy and paving the way for a more inclusive future. Despite the systemic barriers, they innovate, adapt, and build successful enterprises, demonstrating the immense potential that could be unlocked with equitable access to resources and opportunities.

Technology as a Catalyst for Equality

Artificial intelligence represents a powerful opportunity to level the playing field for African American entrepreneurs, providing the tools to overcome many traditional barriers. AI can help entrepreneurs access advanced analytics and automation capabilities previously reserved for large corporations. AI-driven insights can transform how businesses operate, providing the kind of market analysis and operational efficiencies that are key to competitive advantage. It can deliver valuable insights into consumer behavior, optimize business operations, and personalize customer experiences – all of which are essential for driving efficiency and profitability.

However, realizing the full potential of AI for African American entrepreneurs means overcoming nuanced barriers rooted in the digital divide. Access to AI tools often demands significant computing power and specialized knowledge, which may be out of reach for many. Many entrepreneurs find themselves unable to afford the requisite infrastructure – high-speed internet, modern computers, or access to cloud computing services – needed to effectively use AI tools. The disparity in internet access further exacerbates this challenge, as issues with connectivity and quality can hinder full participation in the digital economy – particularly in urban neighborhoods with unreliable service and rural areas lacking broadband infrastructure.

Efforts to bridge the digital divide must focus on both access and capability – ensuring African American entrepreneurs not only possess the technological tools but also have the knowledge to engage with them fully. Initiatives that provide affordable internet access, digital literacy programs, and increased availability of technological resources through community tech hubs are critical components of bridging this gap. Empowering African American communities to fully utilize AI technology also requires culturally responsive training programs that understand the specific barriers these communities face and tailor solutions accordingly.

Building Technological Ecosystems in Underserved Communities

To ensure equal access to the tools needed for success in an AI-driven economy, it is essential to build supportive local ecosystems. Community tech hubs can serve as incubators for African American entrepreneurs, offering high-speed internet, AI tools, and collaborative workspaces that foster innovation. These hubs also provide a space for peer learning and networking, which are crucial for collective advancement. By bringing together individuals with similar goals and challenges, these tech hubs create an environment where shared knowledge and mutual support can flourish.

Historically Black colleges and universities (HBCUs) are uniquely positioned to play a pivotal role in these ecosystems. By aligning AI-focused programs with the specific economic needs of their communities, HBCUs can become centers of technological innovation. HBCUs have historically been pillars of empowerment and education for African Americans, and their role is expanding as technology reshapes economies. Through partnerships with local businesses, they can provide skilled talent, research opportunities, and access to technical resources – directly contributing to the development of vibrant entrepreneurial environments. HBCUs can also offer tailored AI courses and professional certifications that provide African American students with a competitive edge in the tech industry.

Creating Ethical AI for Marginalized Communities

AI can be a powerful tool to address systemic inequities, but only if it is developed with marginalized communities in mind. African American entrepreneurs, informed by their lived experiences, are uniquely equipped to create AI solutions that prioritize fairness and inclusion. AI has the potential to redress some of society's deep-rooted inequities – such as improving access to financial services through equitable credit scoring algorithms or addressing healthcare disparities with diagnostic tools designed for underserved populations. For instance, an AI tool designed with community health needs in mind could help address the racial disparities in healthcare by taking into account cultural and socioeconomic factors often overlooked by traditional systems.

By embedding ethical considerations into their innovations, African American entrepreneurs can ensure that AI serves as a force for good, rather than perpetuating harmful biases. Ethical AI development means actively seeking to eliminate bias in algorithms and involving diverse voices in AI creation. Creating AI systems that are transparent and accountable will also be critical to ensuring they do not harm the communities they intend to serve. By fostering diversity in AI design and testing, entrepreneurs can develop tools that are not only effective but also equitable.

Empowering Through Policy and Advocacy

Public policy plays a crucial role in bridging the equity gap, providing African American entrepreneurs with the opportunity to advocate for systemic change. Policies that increase funding for minority-owned startups or offer tax incentives for investments in underserved communities can foster greater inclusion. Public funding initiatives can help level the playing field, enabling African American entrepreneurs to compete in industries where they have been historically underrepresented. Collaborating with advocacy organizations to push for transparency and accountability in AI systems will help ensure equitable access to technology while protecting vulnerable communities from biased systems.

Moreover, AI literacy is essential for closing the knowledge gap. Programs tailored to African American communities must go beyond technical skills to include a deeper understanding of AI – how it operates, its limitations, and its societal impact. This knowledge will empower entrepreneurs to make informed decisions about integrating AI into their businesses, driving both economic growth and social progress. By understanding how AI systems can both solve problems and create new challenges, African American entrepreneurs can use this technology to make meaningful, community-focused impacts.

Resilience and Adaptability: Learning from History

African American entrepreneurs have long embodied resilience in the face of adversity. From the thriving "Black Wall Street" in Tulsa's Greenwood District to the emergence of today's Black-owned tech startups, African American entrepreneurship has consistently demonstrated adaptability and innovation. The history of Black Wall Street remains a testament to what can be accomplished when communities are given the opportunity to thrive. The district's destruction also serves as a reminder of the resilience required to rebuild and adapt in the face of systemic racism and violence.

This legacy of resilience is especially relevant in the rapidly evolving AI era, where adaptability is key to success. The ability to pivot, to learn, and to develop new skills will determine who thrives as industries evolve. By leveraging their unique perspectives and experiences, African American entrepreneurs can develop AI solutions that drive not only economic success but also positive social impact. Their insights are vital in shaping AI that is responsive to the needs of marginalized communities and in driving innovation that is rooted in equity and justice.

Initiatives and Programs Enhancing Tech Accessibility

Numerous initiatives have emerged to enhance technological accessibility for African American entrepreneurs. Government grants and subsidies provide financial support to help minority-owned businesses acquire digital tools. This support is critical for bridging the capital gap and ensuring that African American entrepreneurs can afford the technologies necessary for growth. Community tech hubs offer free or affordable access to high-speed internet and modern computing resources, reducing barriers to entry and providing access to the digital infrastructure needed to compete.

Partnerships with technology companies also play a significant role in enhancing access. By offering software, training, and support, these companies can help level the playing field. Educational programs and bootcamps, focusing on coding, digital marketing, and other essential skills, further equip African American entrepreneurs with the tools they need to succeed in the digital age. These programs also serve to demystify technology, making AI and other advanced tools more accessible to a broader audience.

Empowering Minority Entrepreneurs with AI: Success Stories

The empowerment potential of AI is vividly illustrated by several success stories across the country. In the Midwest, an African American entrepreneur used AI to optimize precision agriculture, resulting in increased crop yields and improved sustainability. This innovation not only improved the business's bottom line but also contributed to food security in local communities. In the South, a group of educators developed an AI-based platform that adapts to students' learning styles, helping to close the achievement gap in underperforming schools. This project has had a significant impact on young learners, particularly those from marginalized backgrounds who benefit from personalized learning approaches.

Meanwhile, on the East Coast, a minority-owned retail startup used AI for inventory management, significantly reducing costs and enhancing customer satisfaction. This entrepreneur used predictive analytics to manage stock more effectively, demonstrating how AI can drive operational efficiency even in small businesses. These examples demonstrate that AI is not just a business tool – it is a catalyst for social and economic equity. By leveraging AI, African American entrepreneurs can solve community-specific challenges, promote sustainability, and enhance educational outcomes, ultimately contributing to broader societal progress.

Funding Options in the AI Era

Access to funding is a critical element for entrepreneurial success. In the AI era, African American entrepreneurs have a range of funding options, including venture capital, AI-specific grants, and crowdfunding. Traditional venture capital remains difficult to access, but recent years have seen an increase in funds specifically targeted at minority entrepreneurs, which aim to address the disparity in investment. AI-specific grants from public and private organizations provide funding opportunities that encourage innovation in AI solutions that address social and community needs.

Securing investment requires strategic efforts – from building strong networks within the tech community to crafting compelling pitches that underscore the value and problem-solving potential of AI-driven solutions. Participating in pitch competitions and building relationships with investors who understand the importance of diversity can open doors to funding opportunities. Leveraging incubators and accelerators provides not only funding but also mentorship, guidance, and other valuable resources to help scale AI startups. These programs can be particularly beneficial for African American entrepreneurs who may not have access to traditional business networks.

Advocating for Inclusive Tech Policies

Advocacy for inclusive tech policies is essential for ensuring that the benefits of AI and digital technology are accessible to all, including African American entrepreneurs. This includes promoting diversity in the tech sector, ensuring equitable access to data for AI development, and protecting privacy rights, especially for communities vulnerable to surveillance and data misuse. Public policy must include safeguards against the misuse of data and AI technologies that could further marginalize Black communities. It is essential to advocate for policies that support data transparency, privacy, and the ethical use of AI.

Governments and NGOs also play a critical role by providing grants, supporting educational programs, and fostering public–private partnerships to promote inclusive innovation. NGOs, in particular, can work on the ground to ensure that resources reach the communities most in need, bridging the gap between high-level policy and practical, on-the-ground impact. By building coalitions of stakeholders across sectors, we can advocate for inclusive tech policies that ensure technology serves everyone fairly.

Building Strong Entrepreneurial Networks and Mentorship Systems

Strong entrepreneurial networks are the backbone of any thriving business community. For African American entrepreneurs, these networks are vital for collaboration, resource sharing, and mutual support. Local business associations, online communities, and networking events offer essential platforms for connection and growth. Peer-to-peer networking can help African American entrepreneurs overcome isolation, providing opportunities to share strategies, experiences, and encouragement.

Mentorship is equally crucial, providing guidance from experienced entrepreneurs to those just starting their journey. Access to mentorship helps new business owners navigate the complexities of entrepreneurship, including financial planning, marketing, and growth strategies. Support groups and educational resources foster a sense of community and offer practical advice for navigating the challenges of entrepreneurship. Connecting aspiring entrepreneurs with successful business leaders in their communities can serve as an inspiration and provide the hands-on guidance necessary for business success.

Looking Forward: A Collaborative Future

Bridging the gap for African American entrepreneurs requires a collective effort that involves government, industry, and community stakeholders. By fostering partnerships across sectors and leveraging AI as a tool for empowerment, African American entrepreneurs can create a future where technology serves everyone equally. This collaborative vision is not just aspirational – it is essential for addressing the systemic challenges that have historically excluded marginalized communities from the full benefits of economic progress. Collaboration between government entities, private sector leaders, and community organizations can create a more integrated support system that effectively addresses the needs of African American entrepreneurs.

The journey toward inclusive innovation is led by African American entrepreneurs working tirelessly to overcome historical and systemic barriers that have hindered equal opportunity in business. Their journey is characterized by resilience, adaptability, and the relentless pursuit of knowledge and resources. As we look ahead, we envision a future where African American entrepreneurship flourishes, free from the constraints of past biases. In this future, technology becomes the great equalizer – providing access to markets, capital, and networks that were once out of reach. AI and digital tools serve as catalysts for innovation, enabling entrepreneurs to create solutions that drive both economic growth and social equity.

Ultimately, our goal is a diverse entrepreneurial landscape where success is determined by talent and determination, rather than by race or background. In this envisioned future, African American entrepreneurs are not just participants but leaders – shaping technology into a force that benefits all of society. The pursuit of equity in AI and technology is an ongoing mission, one that will require unwavering commitment, collaboration, and advocacy. By continuing to support African American entrepreneurs, we can ensure that the next era of technological advancement is one defined by inclusivity, equity, and shared prosperity for all.

Inspiration Bite: Rediet Abebe

Dr. Rediet Abebe is an Ethiopian computer scientist and co-founder of Mechanism Design for Social Good (MD4SG), an initiative that applies algorithmic tools to address social challenges such as inequality and access to opportunity. Her research intersects algorithms, AI, and social welfare, aiming to create equitable and socially responsible AI systems. Dr. Abebe's work has been recognized for its innovative approach to leveraging AI for social impact, addressing systemic barriers to equitable progress.

Source: https://africans-in-america.com/2021/06/28/rediet-abebe-the-ethiopian-born-computer-scientist-who-is-using-artificial-intelligence-for-social-good/

Reflection Prompts

How can systemic barriers be transformed into opportunities for innovation and advocacy in your entrepreneurial journey?

What alliances or partnerships could you form to address the structural inequities you face?

DSTIf you could design one AI tool to dismantle a systemic barrier, what would it address, and how would it work?

Chapter 4

The Digital Divide

> If someone is blocking your ideas and advancement, find a different way to expose your proposals, innovations and request. There is often someone at the next level or an associate manager that is willing to listen. To break through, you often have to be better than the rest. This takes a lot of work, but it is achievable. – Mark Dean, computer scientist and engineer, chief engineer of the original IBM PC.

The concept of the digital divide has evolved considerably since it first emerged as a term for disparities in access to computers and the internet. In today's era of Artificial Intelligence (AI), this divide has taken on deeper, more nuanced meanings. This chapter examines the complexities of the digital divide, focusing on how it affects African American entrepreneurs in the AI space, and suggests pathways to ensure equitable access to the transformative power of AI for everyone.

AgroLink AI: Empowering Farmers Through Technology

Keyera Shorter's AgroLink AI transformed the fate of Black farmers in rural Georgia by merging modern technology with deep-rooted farming traditions. Leveraging AI, her platform analyzed soil quality, climatic data, and historical crop yields to recommend optimal planting and harvesting times, empowering farmers to make informed decisions that significantly boosted their productivity. But AgroLink AI went beyond providing farming insights – it bridged the gap between rural growers and urban buyers by creating a smart marketplace. The AI matched produce supply with demand by anticipating consumer preferences and local market trends, allowing farmers to set competitive prices. In doing so, Keyera not only revitalized local agriculture but also crafted a self-sustaining ecosystem that gave marginalized farmers a fighting chance in a global market where they were traditionally overlooked. AgroLink AI proved that with the right tools, local knowledge could be amplified to create economic prosperity and technological inclusion for communities often left behind by modern innovation.

AI Empowered, 37–48

doi:10.1108/978-1-83662-816-320251005

Defining the Digital Divide: Beyond Access

The digital divide is not merely about having or lacking physical technology; it is a far more intricate issue involving multiple layers of accessibility and utility. To fully understand the barriers involved, it is necessary to consider several intertwined factors.

One key aspect of the divide is access to infrastructure. This includes not only the availability of high-speed internet but also modern computing devices and stable digital networks. In many underserved communities – whether rural or urban – a lack of these basic infrastructural elements continues to hinder access to AI tools and resources. Without reliable access to high-speed internet or up-to-date digital tools, entire communities find themselves at a disadvantage, effectively excluded from participating fully in the opportunities that the digital age offers. This lack of infrastructure means a lack of foundational tools required to build digital skills and use AI applications, making it difficult to gain traction in an increasingly technology-driven economy.

The divide also encompasses digital literacy, which extends beyond basic access. People must have the skills and knowledge to effectively use digital tools and navigate the online world. Such literacy includes understanding how to operate computers, an ability to code, and familiarity with AI concepts, all of which are critical in this digital age. Digital literacy is the foundation upon which other skills are built, allowing individuals to fully engage with and manage technology to improve their lives, their businesses, and their communities. Digital literacy is no longer optional; it is a critical necessity for anyone who wishes to succeed in the modern economy.

Another important dimension is content and representation. The divide often manifests through the type of content accessible to marginalized groups. If digital spaces do not reflect diverse voices and perspectives, they lose relevance and meaning for these communities. The lack of culturally relevant content limits engagement and creates an environment where marginalized communities do not see their experiences represented, leading to lower rates of participation and utilization. This underrepresentation becomes a barrier to meaningful inclusion. Equally vital is AI literacy, a relatively new but growing component of the digital divide. AI literacy involves understanding what AI can and cannot do, its implications, and its ethical aspects. Empowering individuals to engage critically with AI means equipping them not only to use AI tools but also to help shape their development and application. Ensuring that diverse communities have a voice in the development and deployment of AI technologies is critical to avoid perpetuating existing biases and creating technologies that reflect a broader range of human experience.

The Historical Roots of the Digital Divide

The origins of the digital divide are deeply embedded in a long history of exclusion and unequal investment in African American communities. Structural inequities stretch back centuries, affecting public infrastructure, education, and economic opportunity. Historically, public infrastructure in many predominantly African American neighborhoods – especially those impacted by redlining – lacked sufficient investment, and this neglect extended to digital infrastructure as well.

Redlining, a discriminatory practice that began in the 1930s, effectively excluded African American communities from the investments needed to build thriving neighborhoods, including investments in public utilities like electricity, water, and later, digital infrastructure. This systemic disenfranchisement has left long-term scars on the development of these communities, leading to gaps in education, housing, and employment that persist today. The impact of these structural inequities has compounded over time, limiting opportunities for African Americans to gain equal access to the technologies that are shaping the 21st century.

As the world shifted into the Information Age in the late 20th century, these disparities widened. African American schools frequently lacked the resources available in wealthier, often predominantly white, school districts. The inequities in access to computers, the internet, and modern digital tools became glaringly apparent, as schools in underfunded districts struggled to offer students the basic technological skills needed to thrive in a rapidly digitizing world. As access to computers and the internet became essential for education and business, many Black communities found themselves unable to keep pace, further entrenching economic disparities. These disparities have created a generational knowledge gap that continues to hinder access to high-paying jobs and entrepreneurial opportunities in technology-driven sectors.

Understanding this historical context is essential for crafting solutions that address not only present disparities but also the deep-seated systemic inequities that continue to shape the digital divide. By acknowledging the legacy of discrimination and exclusion, we can work toward building more inclusive systems that prioritize equity and ensure that African American communities are not left behind in the new digital economy.

Digital Equity and Economic Opportunity

The digital divide is about more than access – it is fundamentally about opportunity. In today's AI-driven economy, digital tools are indispensable for entrepreneurship, education, and employment. For African American entrepreneurs, limited access to advanced technologies such as cloud computing and machine learning restricts their ability to innovate and compete on equal terms.

The lack of digital access also means a lack of access to the wealth of information, data analytics, and marketing tools that are essential for scaling a business in today's market. Entrepreneurs need these technologies to understand consumer behavior, manage logistics, and implement effective marketing strategies. In the absence of these resources, Black-owned businesses may struggle to expand beyond their local communities, missing out on opportunities to compete in broader markets.

Bridging this divide requires far more than just installing internet infrastructure. It involves creating pathways for economic mobility through targeted training, providing necessary resources, and establishing support systems that enable entrepreneurs to harness digital tools. Training programs focused on digital literacy and entrepreneurship are critical, as they can equip individuals with the skills needed to thrive in a competitive marketplace. When African American entrepreneurs gain access to the same technologies as others, they can create new opportunities for growth, innovation, and economic advancement. By fostering a supportive environment that includes mentorship, access to funding, and networking opportunities, we can create the conditions necessary for Black-owned businesses to flourish in the digital age.

Broadband as a Civil Right

In the 21st century, broadband access has become as essential as electricity or clean water. The ability to access high-speed internet has a direct impact on an individual's ability to learn, work, and communicate, making it a critical resource in the modern world. However, millions of African Americans still live in areas where reliable, high-speed internet is unavailable or prohibitively expensive. This lack of access disproportionately affects students, job seekers, and entrepreneurs, thereby perpetuating cycles of economic disparity.

The inability to access reliable broadband services can limit educational outcomes, as students without internet access are unable to complete online assignments, attend virtual classes, or access learning resources that are increasingly available only online. Similarly, job seekers are disadvantaged if they cannot access online job postings, apply for jobs digitally, or participate in virtual interviews. Entrepreneurs are perhaps most affected, as reliable internet is essential for accessing online tools, conducting market research, managing logistics, and communicating with clients.

Viewing broadband as a civil right changes the conversation from one of luxury to necessity. Public policy must prioritize the development and expansion of broadband infrastructure in underserved communities. Government initiatives, such as municipal broadband projects, can help ensure that all communities have access to the internet. Municipal broadband initiatives and subsidies for low-income households can help ensure widespread, affordable internet access. Such measures are critical in leveling the playing field for African American entrepreneurs. Ensuring broadband access is not just about providing a service; it is about dismantling barriers to education, opportunity, and prosperity, and allowing all citizens to fully participate in modern society.

AI and the Evolving Nature of the Digital Divide

The digital divide is also changing in nature as AI technologies become more widespread. Access to data, computing power, and specialized skills is becoming increasingly crucial. As AI is integrated into more aspects of daily life, the gap between those who can fetch these tools and those who cannot is widening. African American entrepreneurs often face significant barriers in acquiring these resources, which further widens the divide.

AI technologies rely heavily on access to large datasets and significant computing power to process these datasets effectively. For small businesses, the financial cost of accessing high-quality datasets and the necessary cloud infrastructure can be prohibitive. Furthermore, specialized AI skills, including data analysis, machine learning, and programming, require education and training that may not be readily available in underserved communities. Without access to these critical elements, Black-owned businesses are at risk of being left out of the AI revolution, which has the potential to transform industries from healthcare to finance.

Addressing this evolving divide requires targeted initiatives, such as subsidized access to AI tools, open data platforms, and affordable cloud services that can help even the playing field. Programs that provide open access to data and cloud-based computing resources can make a significant difference for entrepreneurs who otherwise would not be able to afford these tools. Additionally, partnerships between tech companies, governments, and educational institutions could create AI training programs designed to equip underrepresented communities with the skills they need to thrive in an AI-driven world.

The Education Divide in AI

Education remains a cornerstone of efforts to bridge the digital divide, but quality AI education is not accessible to all. African American students are underrepresented in science, technology, engineering, and mathematics (STEM) fields and often do not have early exposure to AI and related technologies. This educational gap, if unaddressed, threatens to permanently exclude African American students from future opportunities in the AI economy.

AI and data science are fast becoming foundational skills for the jobs of the future. However, the current educational system often fails to provide equitable opportunities for students from marginalized backgrounds. Schools in underfunded districts may lack the resources to offer computer science classes or invest in technology that allows students to explore AI concepts. Without targeted intervention, this educational gap risks becoming a permanent barrier to inclusion in the AI economy.

Addressing this requires a multifaceted approach. After-school coding clubs, AI summer camps, and partnerships between tech companies and schools are all effective ways to introduce young African Americans to AI concepts. These programs can spark interest and build foundational skills that will be crucial in their future careers. Mentorship programs are equally important, as they can provide students with role models and guidance as they navigate the challenges of pursuing careers in technology and AI. Mentors can help demystify the field, offer practical advice, and serve as a source of inspiration for students who may not otherwise see themselves represented in the tech industry.

Community-Led Solutions to the Digital Divide

Communities are at the forefront of the fight to bridge the digital divide. African American entrepreneurs and community leaders are leading grassroots initiatives to expand access to technology and provide essential training. These initiatives play a critical role in overcoming barriers that may otherwise seem insurmountable. For example, local organizations are establishing free Wi-Fi zones, hosting coding workshops, and offering AI literacy programs at community centers. Such initiatives show the power of collective action in addressing inequities and demonstrate that sustainable solutions are possible when community members take charge.

Community-led initiatives also offer culturally relevant solutions that resonate more effectively with local populations. For instance, community leaders understand the specific needs and challenges of their neighborhoods and can design programs that directly address those issues. Local businesses hosting coding workshops or community centers offering AI training can create welcoming environments that encourage participation and foster a sense of belonging. These efforts go beyond merely providing access; they empower individuals to become active participants in the digital economy, turning technology into a tool for social mobility and community development.

Investing in these community-led solutions is essential for a sustainable and inclusive approach to bridging the digital divide. By supporting these efforts, we can ensure that technology becomes an empowering tool for African American entrepreneurs rather than a barrier. Partnerships between local governments, private companies, and nonprofits can amplify the impact of these initiatives, providing the resources and infrastructure needed to scale successful programs.

Policy Interventions: Bridging the Gap at Scale

Bridging the digital divide also requires systemic policy interventions. Federal and state governments have a crucial role in addressing the factors that perpetuate this divide. Policies that focus on expanding broadband infrastructure, incentivizing tech companies to make AI tools affordable, and funding AI research programs at historically Black colleges and universities (HBCUs) can all contribute to bridging the gap.

Investing in HBCUs, for example, can create pathways for African American students to gain advanced skills in AI and computer science, thereby creating a pipeline of talent that can contribute to the tech industry. Similarly, federal grants can be used to expand broadband infrastructure in underserved areas, ensuring that communities have the basic connectivity needed to access digital tools and opportunities. Tax incentives for tech companies can encourage them to offer affordable AI tools and services to small businesses, helping to democratize access to these powerful technologies.

These initiatives require collaboration between government entities, the private sector, and community organizations. Effective policymaking must ensure that investments directly benefit the entrepreneurs and communities most in need, providing them with the tools to succeed in the digital and AI-driven economy. Policies must be designed not only to address immediate needs but also to create long-term change by dismantling systemic barriers and ensuring that underserved communities have the resources they need to thrive.

The Intersection of Race, Technology, and Bias

The digital divide is not solely a matter of access; it is also deeply intertwined with issues of representation. African Americans are significantly underrepresented in the tech industry, and this underrepresentation has profound effects on how technologies are designed and deployed. AI algorithms that are trained on datasets that lack diversity can perpetuate biases, leading to outcomes that may disadvantage marginalized groups.

For instance, facial recognition technologies have been found to have higher error rates when identifying people of color due to nonrepresentative training datasets. These biases can have serious consequences, ranging from wrongful identification in criminal investigations to exclusion from opportunities such as job screenings. As AI becomes increasingly integrated into decision-making processes across various sectors, the lack of diversity in the teams developing these technologies becomes a critical issue.

Increasing African American representation in the development of AI technologies is crucial. Achieving this requires not only broad access to educational opportunities but also systemic changes within tech companies to promote inclusive hiring practices and diversity in leadership positions. Companies must recognize the importance of diverse perspectives in creating technologies that serve all communities fairly. By building inclusive work cultures and committing to equity in hiring and leadership, the tech industry can take meaningful steps toward reducing biases in AI and ensuring that these technologies benefit everyone.

A Path Forward: Closing the Divide

Despite the challenges, progress is being made. Efforts from government initiatives, private companies, and grassroots movements are converging to address inequalities in digital access and opportunity. For African American entrepreneurs, these initiatives represent real opportunities to fully participate in the AI-driven economy.

Continuing to advocate for equitable policies, investing in community-based solutions, and fostering inclusive innovation will be key to bridging the digital divide. When these efforts come to fruition, they will unlock the full potential of African American entrepreneurs, driving economic growth and innovation that will benefit society as a whole for generations to come.

Efforts to close the digital divide must also include an ongoing commitment to evaluating the impact of existing policies and programs. By continually assessing what works and what does not, stakeholders can refine their approaches and ensure that investments lead to meaningful and sustainable change. Collaboration across sectors will be essential, as the challenges presented by the digital divide are too complex to be solved by any one entity alone. When government, industry, and community organizations work together, they can create a robust support network that empowers individuals and fosters a more inclusive digital economy.

The Real Impact on African American Entrepreneurs

The digital divide presents formidable barriers for African American entrepreneurs, particularly those seeking to work with AI. Limited access to high-speed internet, advanced digital tools, and relevant skills creates hurdles that can limit innovation, growth, and competitiveness. Moreover, economic challenges, such as the high costs of acquiring AI technology and training skilled personnel, make it even more difficult for Black-owned startups to thrive.

Access to high-quality technology is not just about equipment or software; it also involves the ability to use these tools effectively to solve business problems, streamline operations, and innovate. For African American entrepreneurs, limited access to these tools can stifle creativity and prevent them from reaching their full potential. The digital divide essentially creates a two-tiered system where those with access to cutting-edge technology can move forward, while those without are left behind, further widening the gap in wealth and opportunity.

Beyond these immediate barriers, African American entrepreneurs often face systemic sociocultural obstacles, such as implicit bias and a lack of representation in the tech industry. These challenges make securing funding, forging partnerships, and accessing critical opportunities all the more difficult. Investors may be hesitant to fund Black-owned tech ventures, not necessarily because of the quality of their ideas, but due to biases and stereotypes that persist within the investment community. Addressing the digital divide in AI thus requires an understanding of both technological and sociocultural dimensions, and an approach that seeks to overcome the broader economic and educational inequities faced by African American entrepreneurs.

Strategies for Inclusion and Empowerment

To bridge this technological chasm, a multifaceted strategy is required. Investments in infrastructure are crucial to expanding broadband and ensuring equitable internet access for underserved communities. Expanding internet access allows individuals and businesses to engage with the digital economy on a level playing field, making it possible to innovate, learn, and grow. Equally important is the enhancement of digital literacy through comprehensive educational programs in schools and community centers. Such programs should not only provide basic skills but also cover advanced topics like coding, data analysis, and AI concepts.

Raising awareness of AI and its implications for society is another vital component. Promoting AI literacy through educational initiatives and public forums can help demystify this technology and encourage critical engagement. By making AI more approachable and less intimidating, individuals who may not have initially considered AI as accessible to them can begin to see its potential. For African American entrepreneurs, targeted support, such as mentorship programs, access to capital, and training, can provide the necessary resources to compete and succeed. Mentorship is particularly impactful because it not only offers practical guidance but also builds confidence, showing young entrepreneurs that success in the tech industry is attainable.

Creating greater diversity in the tech industry is also essential for meaningful change. This involves addressing barriers in both education and employment, promoting inclusive hiring practices, and fostering environments where African American professionals feel welcomed and supported. Building a diverse workforce requires a commitment to change at all levels, from recruitment to promotion. Companies must actively seek out talent from underrepresented communities and ensure that their work environments are inclusive, where every individual feels that they belong and can contribute fully.

Community-Driven Innovation and Resilience

Despite significant challenges, there are numerous examples of African American entrepreneurs overcoming the digital divide through resilience, innovation, and community support. Entrepreneurs like Antonio Wells and Jewel Burks Solomon have built successful tech ventures from the ground up, offering powerful examples of how, with the right resources and support, the digital divide can be overcome. These stories serve as an inspiration, demonstrating what is possible when systemic barriers are challenged.

Community support is often a key factor in these success stories. African American entrepreneurs who receive encouragement from their communities are more likely to persist in the face of adversity, finding creative solutions to overcome the barriers they encounter. By creating networks of support, from local tech hubs to mentorship programs, communities can play a pivotal role in fostering innovation and growth. When communities rally behind their entrepreneurs, they create fertile ground for new ideas, collaboration, and shared success.

The Role of Education in Bridging the Divide

Education remains a critical component in closing the digital divide and enabling African American entrepreneurs to succeed in the AI era. Enhancing tech literacy and skills across all levels of education is vital to ensuring equitable participation in the digital economy. This means integrating digital literacy into school curriculums, providing professional development for teachers, and setting up community-based programs to support lifelong learning.

Teachers play a crucial role in shaping how students perceive and interact with technology. Professional development programs that equip educators with the knowledge and tools to teach digital literacy effectively are essential. Teachers must feel confident in their ability to guide students through the complexities of technology and AI, and they need the resources to keep up with the rapidly evolving landscape of digital education. Community-based programs also play a key role, particularly for adult learners who may have missed out on digital literacy education in school. These programs offer an opportunity for lifelong learning, helping individuals stay competitive in a changing job market.

Building the Infrastructure for Inclusion

Closing the digital divide also depends heavily on the development of robust digital infrastructure. Investments in high-speed internet, data centers, and mobile networks must be made to ensure that all communities, especially underserved and rural areas, have the same opportunities for participation in the digital economy. Public and private partnerships can play a significant role in this regard, with governments providing incentives and subsidies and private companies contributing through direct investments and social responsibility initiatives.

The expansion of mobile networks is particularly important in rural areas where traditional broadband infrastructure may be challenging to deploy. Mobile technology offers a flexible solution that can connect remote communities to the broader digital world. Similarly, investing in local data centers can reduce latency and improve the overall quality of internet services, making it easier for businesses to operate efficiently. These investments must be complemented by efforts to make technology affordable, ensuring that high-speed internet and modern devices are within reach for all members of society, regardless of income.

Advocacy and Policy Interventions

Effective advocacy for equitable tech policy is essential to promote shared benefits of technology. Organizations like the Kapor Center are already leading the charge, working toward expanded access, increased tech accountability, and greater investment in digital infrastructure. Grassroots organizations and professional networks are also playing important roles by pushing for equitable hiring practices and systemic changes within the tech industry.

Advocacy efforts must be rooted in a clear understanding of the specific challenges faced by marginalized communities. By collecting data, sharing stories, and highlighting the human impact of the digital divide, advocacy organizations can influence policymakers to make informed decisions. These policies must aim at creating systemic changes that addresses the root causes of inequity, such as lack of investment in underserved communities and barriers to education and employment. The goal is to create a technological landscape that is inclusive, fair, and accessible to all.

Grassroots Movements and Community Tech Hubs

Local initiatives are critical in closing the digital divide from the bottom up. Grassroots movements and community tech hubs serve as vital resources for communities, offering access to internet, equipment, and educational programs. By tailoring solutions to the unique needs of local populations, these initiatives ensure that technology serves as a bridge rather than a barrier.

Community tech hubs provide more than just internet access; they serve as gathering places where people can learn, collaborate, and innovate. They offer educational workshops, mentoring opportunities, and a supportive environment for aspiring entrepreneurs. By creating spaces where individuals feel comfortable exploring technology, community tech hubs help break down the intimidation factor that often comes with learning new digital skills. They foster a culture of curiosity and creativity, empowering individuals to see themselves as capable tech users and innovators.

Grassroots movements also play a crucial role in advocating for policy change at the local level. Community organizers can effectively voice the needs of their neighborhoods, ensuring that local governments prioritize investments in digital infrastructure and education. These movements are characterized by their adaptability and responsiveness, often providing immediate solutions to pressing problems while advocating for longer-term systemic changes.

Hope on the Horizon

Though the digital divide remains a significant challenge, there is hope. With government programs, private sector initiatives, and community-driven movements all working toward reducing disparities in digital access, real progress is being made. For African American entrepreneurs, these collective efforts signify more than just access to technology; they represent an opportunity to fully participate and lead in the AI-driven future.

Continuing to invest in community-led solutions, fostering inclusive policies, and ensuring equitable representation in the tech industry are key to overcoming the divide. With sustained effort and collaboration, we can unlock the full economic and social potential of African American entrepreneurs, driving innovation, growth, and progress for generations to come.

The road ahead will require perseverance, creativity, and collective action. It will require all stakeholders – government, businesses, educators, and community leaders – to work together to dismantle the barriers that have held back too many for too long. By bridging the digital divide, we are not only creating opportunities for individuals; we are also building a more inclusive and innovative society that benefits everyone. The progress we make today will set the foundation for future generations to thrive in an increasingly digital and interconnected world.

Inspiration Bite: Brandon Anderson

Brandon Anderson is the founder of Raheem.ai, a chatbot designed to collect and analyze data on police interactions, particularly focusing on incidents of misconduct. By leveraging AI, Raheem.ai empowers communities, especially those marginalized, to report and address police violence, thereby bridging the digital divide in civic engagement and accountability. Anderson's work exemplifies the use of AI to amplify voices and experiences that are often overlooked, fostering greater transparency and justice.

Source: https://civic-hackers.org/2017-civic-hacker-summit-archive/raheem-ai-police-accountability-engine/

Reflection Prompts

In a world where digital access is as vital as clean water, what role can you play in ensuring equitable access for your community?

How can you leverage AI and digital tools to create scalable solutions that bridge gaps in education, health, or commerce?

Imagine your business thriving in a future where the digital divide no longer exists – what would that look like, and how can you help realize it?

Chapter 5

Innovation at the Margins

> Artificial intelligence will reach human levels by around 2029. Follow that out further to 2045, we will have multiplied the intelligence, the human biological machine intelligence of our civilization, a billion-fold. – Ray Kurzweil

The contributions of African American entrepreneurs to the field of technology are often unsung, their stories hidden beneath mainstream narratives. This chapter seeks to illuminate these innovators – the hidden gems who, despite systemic barriers, have emerged as pioneers in the Artificial Intelligence (AI) revolution. We explore their inspiring journeys, the unique challenges they have overcome, and the groundbreaking innovations they have brought to the world. By unraveling their stories, we can better appreciate the intersection of resilience, creativity, and technology that characterizes their contributions. These narratives serve as powerful reminders of the human spirit's ability to transcend barriers and influence the very core of technological progress.

Crowdfunding Corp: Community Entrepreneurship Reimagined

Crowdfunding Corp envisioned a future where entrepreneurial funding was driven by collective empowerment rather than institutional gatekeeping. Crowdfunding Corp was founded, an AI-powered crowdfunding platform that assessed community needs and identified high-impact ideas led by African American innovators. By analyzing social sentiment data and demographic trends, Crowdfunding Corp ensured that every contribution was channeled to ventures with the potential for the greatest community impact. Crowdfunding Corp's platform employed natural language processing to highlight community-driven narratives, turning underrepresented entrepreneurs into compelling storytellers capable of attracting the funding they needed. Crowdfunding Corp didn't just provide money – it fostered a culture of mutual investment and empowerment, transforming community members into stakeholders of local success stories. By emphasizing frugal innovation and pooling community resources, Crowdfunding Corp's platform redefined how marginalized

AI Empowered, 49–60

Published under exclusive licence by Emerald Publishing Limited
doi:10.1108/978-1-83662-816-320251006

groups could self-finance projects that uplifted entire neighborhoods, breaking the traditional cycle of relying on external, often biased, funding bodies.

Disruptive Innovation From the Margins

Innovation from the margins often arises from necessity and an intimate understanding of overlooked needs. African American entrepreneurs have historically been at the forefront of such disruptive changes, creating solutions that cater to underserved communities. Community-focused fintech platforms, for example, have been developed to address long-standing inequities in banking and lending systems. By leveraging AI, these platforms ensure fair credit assessments, dismantling systemic biases that have excluded many from economic opportunities.

The ability to identify gaps in mainstream markets has enabled African American entrepreneurs to redefine traditional business models through AI. Whether it's integrating predictive analytics into small-scale retail operations or developing AI-driven platforms for local artists, these innovators have revolutionized how communities engage with technology and culture. Their work is reshaping industries from the ground up, proving that disruptive innovation can thrive in the margins of society.

The transformative potential of such grassroots innovation cannot be understated. The ingenuity seen in marginalized communities speaks to a broader truth: the power of necessity as a catalyst for invention. Historically, African American entrepreneurs have been more attuned to the needs of underserved populations and have employed creative problem-solving approaches to develop customized solutions. This unique perspective has led to breakthrough technologies that, while initially intended to serve specific community needs, have gained traction in mainstream markets, often leading to broader societal impacts. Their efforts showcase the potential for technology to empower rather than alienate, creating systems that work for all individuals, regardless of their background.

The Role of Grassroots Innovation

Often underestimated in conversations about AI and entrepreneurship, grassroots innovation plays a critical role in driving local-level change. For African American entrepreneurs, grassroots efforts often mean using AI to address hyper-local issues – such as optimizing public transportation in underserved neighborhoods or creating real-time community resource-sharing tools during crises. This approach to innovation ensures that technological progress is equitable, extending benefits to those who need it most.

By creating scalable solutions rooted in the specific needs of local contexts, entrepreneurs at the margins bridge the gap between technological advancement and community empowerment. Grassroots innovation democratizes technology, transforming it from a luxury of the privileged into a tool for widespread societal improvement. Through these efforts, African American entrepreneurs redefine what it means to create impact – by making technology accessible, actionable, and beneficial for their communities.

The impact of grassroots innovation is profound, as it brings real change where it is most needed. Unlike top-down approaches, which often miss the nuances of local needs, grassroots innovation offers a finely tuned, context-sensitive approach that genuinely improves quality of life. This type of innovation encourages a participatory model, involving community members directly in the design and implementation of solutions. In doing so, it also fosters a sense of ownership and empowerment within the community, as they see themselves not just as recipients of technological advancements but as active participants in their creation. The result is a powerful, sustainable cycle of innovation that can uplift entire neighborhoods, giving rise to long-term socioeconomic benefits.

Creative Industries and AI: A Cultural Revolution

African American entrepreneurs are uniquely positioned to lead the integration of AI into creative industries, harnessing technology to amplify cultural expression. Generative AI tools now enable artists to compose music, design visual art, and produce films with unprecedented efficiency and reach. This transformation is more than just a technological shift; it is a cultural revolution, one that redefines the relationship between creativity and technology.

This movement is about more than automation – it is about storytelling, representation, and heritage. Through AI, African American entrepreneurs are preserving and sharing cultural narratives, from creating virtual reality experiences that bring historical events to life, to developing voice recognition systems that celebrate and understand African American Vernacular English (AAVE). These innovations illustrate how culture and technology can coexist and thrive, ensuring that diverse voices are heard, celebrated, and preserved.

The cultural revolution powered by AI opens new possibilities for representation in media, art, and education. It empowers creators to tell stories that have long been ignored or misrepresented in mainstream narratives. By harnessing AI tools, African American artists can control the narrative, producing content that reflects their experiences authentically. This is particularly powerful in a society where the cultural contributions of marginalized communities have often been co-opted without due recognition. The integration of AI into creative fields allows for greater agency and visibility, transforming cultural products into a medium for activism, education, and unity.

Moreover, AI's role in preserving cultural heritage is crucial in this age of rapid digitalization. African American entrepreneurs are taking strides to create digital archives, immersive learning experiences, and tools that make historical and cultural information more accessible. This work is not just about preserving the past; it is about empowering future generations with knowledge and pride in their cultural identity. By employing technology to bridge the gap between the past and the future, African American innovators are ensuring that the cultural wealth of their community is both preserved and evolved in new, dynamic forms.

Resilience Through Adaptive Technologies

Adaptive technologies powered by AI are transforming business operations, especially for African American entrepreneurs navigating systemic challenges. AI-driven customer support systems, for instance, help small businesses scale their operations without extensive resources. Similarly, machine learning algorithms optimize supply chain logistics, enabling emerging enterprises to operate more efficiently.

These technologies serve as a form of resilience, allowing entrepreneurs to adapt to changing market conditions and compete with larger, established players. By leveraging AI, African American entrepreneurs are overcoming operational inefficiencies and breaking down barriers that have historically limited their growth. Adaptive technologies are thus not only tools for business efficiency but also symbols of perseverance, enabling these entrepreneurs to thrive even in resource-constrained environments.

Resilience through adaptive technologies also entails an ongoing learning process. Entrepreneurs are using AI to gather insights on consumer preferences, market dynamics, and operational efficiencies. These insights allow them to be agile, responding quickly to challenges while capitalizing on emerging opportunities. For many African American business owners, technology has become the equalizer – a way to compete in a market that has often been structurally skewed against them. By adopting these advanced tools, they are not only keeping pace with industry standards but are also setting new benchmarks for operational excellence and customer satisfaction.

Adaptive technologies also help in overcoming geographic and financial barriers that might otherwise restrict growth. Virtual assistants, automated inventory management, and AI-powered financial tools mean that a business can effectively scale without needing the same physical presence or capital as larger competitors. In this way, technology becomes a means of leveling the playing field, enabling small businesses to punch above their weight and sustain their growth trajectories even in the face of adversity.

Collaboration as a Catalyst for Innovation

Innovation at the margins is rarely a solo endeavor. Collaboration is essential for pooling resources, sharing knowledge, and scaling impact. African American entrepreneurs benefit from building networks with research institutions, tech companies, and community organizations that share a commitment to inclusive innovation.

Partnerships HBCUs could foster research in AI applications tailored to underserved communities. Collaborations with larger tech firms provide access to advanced tools, mentorship, and opportunities for growth. Such partnerships amplify the potential of innovations emerging from the margins, helping transform them from local solutions into catalysts for broad societal change.

Collaboration also brings an infusion of new ideas and cross-disciplinary knowledge that can elevate an innovative concept from good to groundbreaking.

African American entrepreneurs have often found strength in numbers, forming collectives and collaborative ventures that allow for shared risk and distributed expertise. Such networks have proven invaluable for scaling technological innovations that might otherwise struggle to find the support needed to expand.

Moreover, collaboration with community organizations ensures that technological innovations are rooted in real, everyday challenges. By involving community stakeholders in the design and implementation process, African American entrepreneurs are not only creating better products but also nurturing trust and adoption of these solutions. These collaborative approaches make technology more sustainable and ensure it has a lasting, positive impact.

Overcoming Market Barriers With AI

Breaking into mainstream markets remains a significant challenge for African American entrepreneurs. AI can be a game changer in leveling the playing field. Predictive analytics help identify emerging trends, enabling businesses to strategically position themselves ahead of competitors. Additionally, AI-powered marketing tools allow entrepreneurs to target specific demographics effectively, reducing the cost of customer acquisition.

By using AI for market insights, process automation, and enhanced decision-making, African American entrepreneurs can overcome traditional barriers and establish a foothold in highly competitive industries. The integration of AI is not just about survival; it's about setting up presence, influence, and the power to reshape industries from within.

AI-driven market intelligence provides smaller enterprises with an edge that was previously out of reach. Entrepreneurs can use these tools to understand customer behavior, identify new market niches, and refine their offerings based on precise, data-driven insights. These capabilities are crucial in navigating industries that have traditionally been inaccessible due to high barriers to entry. With AI's analytical power, African American entrepreneurs are making strategic, informed decisions that enhance their competitiveness, transforming their market positioning from reactive to proactive.

AI also supports more sophisticated customer engagement strategies. Through AI-driven chatbots, personalized recommendations, and targeted advertising campaigns, entrepreneurs can build and maintain strong customer relationships at a fraction of the traditional cost. These tools allow for a level of personalization and responsiveness that was once only feasible for larger corporations, giving smaller businesses the opportunity to compete on a more even playing field. By employing AI to enhance customer experiences, African American entrepreneurs are not only building brand loyalty but also redefining consumer expectations.

Human-Centric AI: Designing for Impact

For African American entrepreneurs, innovation is often about more than profit: it is about creating meaningful change. Human-centric AI, which prioritizes user needs and ethical considerations, aligns with this goal. Increasingly, these entrepreneurs are designing AI solutions that address social inequities, such as healthcare access, educational disparities, and housing challenges.

These efforts prove that technology can be a force for good when developed with empathy and purpose. By centering human experiences in AI design, African American innovators are leading a shift toward more inclusive and impactful technologies, solutions that not only advance industries but also contribute to societal well-being.

Human-centric AI focuses on making technology work for people, rather than the other way around. By designing with the user in mind, African American entrepreneurs ensure that their innovations meet the real needs of the communities they serve. This approach leads to the development of solutions that are intuitive, accessible, and relevant. For example, AI-driven healthcare platforms developed by African American entrepreneurs often incorporate culturally relevant insights, making them more effective for marginalized populations whose needs are not adequately addressed by mainstream solutions.

Additionally, human-centric AI involves an ethical commitment to mitigating biases within algorithms. African American entrepreneurs are uniquely positioned to recognize and address biases that exist within many AI models. By advocating for fairness and transparency, they are contributing to the development of AI systems that are more equitable and just. Their work is a reminder that technology should serve humanity and that ethical innovation is key to creating tools that uplift rather than marginalize.

Scaling Innovation From the Margins

Scaling innovation from the margins to the mainstream is a unique challenge, but one that African American entrepreneurs are increasingly overcoming. Success stories abound of startups that began addressing local issues before expanding nationally or even globally, using AI to achieve scalability and reach.

Scaling requires more than just funding; it involves building a robust team, creating meaningful partnerships, and keeping the integrity of the original mission. For African American entrepreneurs, maintaining this balance is crucial to ensure that their innovations remain impactful and inclusive, even as they grow. The journey from the local to the global is not only about scale but it is also about preserving the spirit of community-focused innovation that defined their beginnings.

One of the most significant aspects of scaling is the challenge of retaining the original vision while expanding reach. African American entrepreneurs often build their businesses with community empowerment at the core, and as they grow, there is a risk of that vision being diluted. However, the stories of those who have succeeded in scaling show a commitment to their foundational values: that is, an assurance that growth does not come at the expense of the community.

Scaling also means adapting to new markets without losing authenticity. Entrepreneurs must navigate different regulatory environments, consumer expectations, and market dynamics while staying true to the purpose that drove their initial success. African American entrepreneurs who successfully scale their innovations bring a unique voice to broader markets, enriching industries with perspectives that have often been missing. They serve as role models for others, demonstrating that it is possible to grow a business in a way that remains true to its roots and its community.

The Future of Marginalized Innovators

The future holds immense promise for innovators operating at the margins. As AI continues to evolve, African American entrepreneurs are poised to harness emerging technologies like edge computing, blockchain integration, and quantum machine learning to create groundbreaking solutions. Their unique perspectives, shaped by lived experiences, position them to identify opportunities that others might overlook, driving innovation that benefits both their communities and society as a whole.

By fostering a culture that values diversity, collaboration, and creativity, we can ensure that innovation from the margins remains a powerful force in shaping the future of technology. As these entrepreneurs continue to break barriers, their contributions will not only advance AI but also help build a world where technology serves everyone, equitably and inclusively.

As technology continues to transform industries and reshape societies, the contributions of marginalized innovators will become increasingly vital. Their capacity to view challenges through a lens shaped by lived experiences provides them with a unique advantage. This ability to empathize and design with diverse end-users in mind ensures that the technologies developed are not only innovative but also socially relevant and impactful. As African American entrepreneurs embrace and integrate emerging technologies, they stand ready to influence the trajectory of AI in a way that promotes justice, inclusion, and opportunity for all.

The next wave of innovation will likely see African American entrepreneurs at the forefront of transformative technological applications. With increased access to venture capital, mentorship, and collaborative ecosystems, these entrepreneurs will be well-positioned to scale their innovations globally. The broader tech industry stands to benefit immensely from their involvement, as it moves toward more holistic, inclusive approaches to problem-solving. By championing the contributions of African American innovators, we can collectively build a future where technology is not just a tool for profit but a catalyst for societal good.

Unveiling Hidden Gems: African American Tech Entrepreneurs

The tech industry, despite its image of progress and inclusivity, has often marginalized the contributions of African Americans. Yet, Black entrepreneurs have consistently been at the forefront of technological innovation, creating solutions that address real-world problems and challenge the status quo. Their stories are not just tales of individual achievement but also testaments to the resilience and creativity of the African American community.

The hidden gems of the tech industry are those individuals whose innovations have laid the groundwork for significant advancements, even if their names have not always received widespread recognition. These entrepreneurs often operate behind the scenes, making invaluable contributions to the functionality and efficiency of modern technologies. Their persistence and ingenuity drive them to continue breaking barriers, forging a path for others to follow. These stories highlight the importance of recognizing and uplifting underrepresented voices in tech, as they often bring fresh perspectives that can lead to the most profound breakthroughs.

Defining Success: Beyond Financial Metrics

Success in the African American business context is multifaceted. It is measured not solely by financial gains but by the impact on the community, the ability to inspire the next generation, and the breaking of barriers that have historically impeded progress. African American tech entrepreneurs define success in terms of:

- Creating inclusive technologies that serve diverse communities.
- Fostering diversity within the tech ecosystem by challenging underrepresentation.
- Paving the way for future innovators by serving as role models and mentors.

Financial success, while important, is often secondary to the broader mission of empowerment, representation, and community upliftment. For these entrepreneurs, building a thriving business is also about ensuring that others can follow in their footsteps. The ripple effect of one person's success can open doors for many others, creating a legacy that extends beyond individual achievement. This holistic view of success challenges the traditional metrics of profit and valuation, instead emphasizing long-term social impact and community development.

Breaking New Ground: Pioneers of AI in the African American Community

The rise of pioneering figures in the African American community, who have embraced AI to drive innovation and progress, represents a significant milestone. These pioneers are not only developing new technologies but also laying groundwork for future generations. By addressing complex social issues like healthcare disparities, educational inequities, and economic injustice, these leaders are transforming communities and industries alike.

These pioneers bring a unique perspective to the AI landscape. They focus on developing solutions that address gaps in existing systems, gaps that often go unnoticed by those not directly affected by them. Whether it's creating AI-driven platforms to improve public health outcomes or designing educational tools that cater to the needs of underserved students, their work is reshaping the narrative of who technology is for and what it can accomplish. The impact of their contributions extends beyond their immediate industries; they are building new paradigms for how AI can be used to solve deeply entrenched social issues.

Innovative Business Models: Emerging from the Margins

From the fringes of the mainstream economy, African American entrepreneurs have emerged with innovative business models that challenge conventional norms. Leveraging AI, they have introduced new ways of delivering products and services that are inclusive and representative of diverse needs. Their business models emphasize community empowerment, sustainability, and social impact, reflecting a commitment to using AI as a force for positive change.

These innovative models often draw inspiration from the resilience and resourcefulness that characterize marginalized communities. The solutions created are inherently practical, designed not only to survive but to thrive amid systemic obstacles. Whether it's creating fintech solutions for underbanked communities, healthcare tools that understand the nuances of different demographics, or platforms that promote local artists and small businesses, African American entrepreneurs are redefining what success looks like. They prove that profitability and social impact are not mutually exclusive; rather, they can enhance each other when innovation is driven by empathy and a genuine desire to solve real problems.

The Power of Representation: Inspiring the Next Generation

Representation is crucial, especially in fields like AI that are shaping the future. African American role models in AI serve as symbols of possibility for aspiring innovators. Their achievements in AI are not only significant for technological advancements but also for the inspiration they provide to the next generation of Black entrepreneurs. The presence of role models ensures that the pathways they forged remain open and accessible for others to follow.

Representation goes beyond mere visibility; it instills confidence and fuels ambition. When young people see successful individuals who look like them and come from similar backgrounds, it becomes easier for them to envision themselves in similar roles. The influence of African American tech entrepreneurs extends far beyond their companies. They speak at schools, mentor young talent, and advocate for inclusive education and policies that create pathways into tech for underserved populations. These efforts ensure that the next generation will be even better equipped to contribute to the AI industry, continuing the legacy of innovation and resilience.

Challenges Turned Opportunities: Adapting and Overcoming

Challenges often serve as a catalyst for innovation. African American tech entrepreneurs have adeptly turned market challenges into opportunities by adapting AI solutions to meet specific needs. By analyzing market trends and consumer behavior through data analytics, these entrepreneurs have developed AI-driven products and services that fill market gaps and provide enhanced value to customers. Their success is rooted in overcoming obstacles with innovative thinking that transforms potential setbacks into steppingstones.

The systemic challenges faced by African American entrepreneurs are significant but not insurmountable. Issues such as limited access to funding, biases within industry networks, and reduced opportunities for visibility require resilience and a willingness to adapt. By turning these obstacles into opportunities for learning and growth, African American entrepreneurs have demonstrated that adversity can be a powerful motivator for innovation. They have built businesses that are not only profitable but also socially conscious, contributing to a broader narrative of progress and empowerment. Their solutions often resonate deeply with underserved markets because they come from a place of shared experience and understanding.

Community and Collaboration: The Power of Networks

Support networks are integral to the entrepreneurial ecosystem, particularly for African American tech entrepreneurs. These networks provide resources, knowledge, and emotional backing, fostering environments where ideas can be nurtured and collaborations can flourish. Partnerships with larger corporations, educational institutions, and government agencies can lead to mutually beneficial outcomes, providing access to new technologies, markets, and funding opportunities. Collaboration is not just a strategy – it is a cornerstone of innovation and resilience.

Community-driven support networks often provide the first level of validation and encouragement that is crucial for any entrepreneur. African American entrepreneurs frequently draw on their local communities, industry mentors, and peer networks to help navigate the complexities of scaling a business. These connections not only provide practical support, such as advice on navigating regulatory requirements or securing funding, but also offer emotional support, helping entrepreneurs to remain resilient in the face of challenges. Such networks transform entrepreneurship from a lonely journey into a collective endeavor, emphasizing the importance of shared success and community upliftment.

Scaling Up: From Startup to Industry Leader

Transitioning from a startup to an industry leader requires strategic growth across multiple facets of business development. For African American entrepreneurs in AI, this involves continuously innovating, diversifying product offerings, acquiring top talent, and identifying new markets. Establishing a strong brand, maintaining customer engagement, and securing funding are crucial steps in this journey. Adaptability is key, along with thought leadership – becoming voices in the industry by contributing to discussions, publishing research, and speaking at conferences.

Scaling up also involves building operational efficiencies that allow for growth without compromising on quality or mission. African American entrepreneurs often face unique challenges in this phase, particularly in accessing the capital required for expansion. However, many have successfully navigated these barriers by leveraging strategic partnerships, grants, and innovative financing models. By doing so, they have expanded their reach and solidified their influence within their respective industries. These entrepreneurs are setting examples for how to scale ethically, ensuring that growth continues to benefit the communities they originally set out to serve.

Celebrating Achievements and Shaping the Future

The achievements of African American entrepreneurs in the AI industry are a testimony to their perseverance, creativity, and pursuit of excellence. They have advanced technological innovation while paving the way for a more inclusive and equitable entrepreneurial landscape. The future of African American entrepreneurship in AI is filled with potential and promise. As the industry continues to evolve, these entrepreneurs will play a pivotal role in shaping its direction, ensuring that technology is created by and for everyone.

With increased access to resources, networks, and support systems, African American entrepreneurs will continue to break new ground, create innovative solutions, and inspire future generations of tech leaders. Their commitment to diversity, equity, and inclusion will enrich the AI ecosystem, leading to a future where technology is an empowering force for all.

The future is about ensuring that the strides made thus far are not just sustained but expanded upon. This means that support from broader society – including policy changes, increased funding opportunities, and a genuine commitment to equity from larger tech firms – is essential. The impact that African American entrepreneurs are having on the tech industry is undeniable, but with greater support, their contributions can be even more transformative. Celebrating their achievements means acknowledging their past struggles, their current successes, and their immense potential to shape the technological landscape of tomorrow.

As we look to the future, it is clear that the role of African American innovators will be central to the ongoing evolution of AI and technology as a whole. By integrating lived experiences with advanced technical knowledge, these entrepreneurs are not only contributing to technological progress but also reshaping the cultural and ethical frameworks within which these technologies operate. Their work ensures that the tech industry evolves in a way that is not just forward-looking but also fair, inclusive, and socially responsible. The potential is limitless, and the time to support and amplify these voices is now.

Inspiration Bite: Joy Buolamwini

Joy Buolamwini is a Ghanaian-American computer scientist and digital activist who founded the Algorithmic Justice League (AJL) in 2016. Her work focuses on uncovering and addressing biases in AI systems, particularly in facial recognition technologies. Buolamwini's research has demonstrated that many AI systems exhibit significant inaccuracies when identifying individuals with darker skin tones and women, leading to broader discussions on ethical AI development. Through AJL, she combines art and research to advocate for equitable and accountable AI, emphasizing the need for transparency and fairness in algorithmic decision-making.

Source: https://www.media.mit.edu/people/joyab/overview/

Reflection Prompts

What constraints or challenges have spurred your creativity or critical thinking skills in the past?

How can you make use of scarce resources or unique perspectives to create innovative solutions?

Who in the African American community inspires you with their ability to innovate against the odds, and what can you learn from them?

Chapter 6

Policy and Progress

> Change will not come if we wait for some other person or if we wait for some other time. – Barack Obama

The journey of African American entrepreneurs in the Artificial Intelligence (AI) industry is deeply entwined with the evolving policy landscape that governs technological innovation and business development. This chapter examines the intricate relationship between historical legislation, contemporary policies, and the distinct challenges faced by minority-owned businesses in the AI sector. We will explore how past policies have influenced the current business climate and assess how today's initiatives are attempting to dismantle the enduring barriers to equitable participation in the AI revolution. The path that African American entrepreneurs have taken in this sector is not just a reflection of personal ambition and innovation but also an indicator of the broader social and political environment that shapes opportunity and equity in technological growth.

PolicyBridge AI: Shaping Policy for Equitable Progress

Recognizing the importance of systemic change, Marcus Jennings launched PolicyBridge AI, an advocacy platform that utilized artificial intelligence to shape public policy toward equitable progress. PolicyBridge AI analyzed legislation, historical policy impacts, and demographic data to identify gaps where marginalized communities were underserved. The platform used predictive modeling to simulate the outcomes of proposed policies, allowing community leaders and policymakers to make data-driven decisions that supported African American entrepreneurs and other marginalized groups. Marcus worked alongside think tanks, community advocates, and lawmakers to create an interface where AI insights were accessible and actionable. By providing clear visualizations of the impacts of policy changes, PolicyBridge AI empowered communities with the knowledge needed to advocate effectively for themselves. Marcus's work underscored the role of technology not only in business but also in creating a just society, where policy could be leveraged to dismantle historical inequities and build a foundation for inclusive economic growth.

AI Empowered, 61–69

Published under exclusive licence by Emerald Publishing Limited
doi:10.1108/978-1-83662-816-320251007

Historical Policy Context

The evolution of African American entrepreneurship in technology has been significantly shaped by a series of legislative efforts aimed at redressing historical inequities and fostering a more inclusive business environment. The Civil Rights Act of 1964, for instance, was a cornerstone that not only sought to end discrimination in broader society but also laid the groundwork for fairer business practices by prohibiting discrimination based on race, color, religion, sex, or national origin. This created an essential legal framework that allowed minority entrepreneurs to pursue opportunities previously denied to them. By ensuring that African American entrepreneurs had a more level playing field, the Act opened the door to wider participation in various economic sectors, including technology.

Subsequent efforts further expanded support for minority businesses. Executive Order 11,625, signed by President Nixon in 1971, aimed specifically at promoting minority business enterprises, focusing on providing technical and management assistance to these entities through the Office of Minority Business Enterprise. This effort highlighted the federal government's growing recognition of the systemic barriers faced by minority entrepreneurs, emphasizing the need for targeted assistance and deliberate intervention to offset historical disadvantages. Later, the Community Reinvestment Act of 1977 sought to address disparities in credit access by encouraging financial institutions to meet the credit needs of all segments of their communities, particularly low- and moderate-income areas often populated by minority groups. This legislation was crucial in mitigating the economic redlining practices that had systematically excluded minority communities from financial services, thus providing more opportunities for African American entrepreneurs to access capital.

Similarly, the Telecommunications Act of 1996 aimed to foster competition and increase access to technology, which was essential for underserved communities entering the rapidly expanding digital era. This Act was a pivotal move to break down monopolies in the telecommunications industry, effectively lowering barriers for new market entrants, including minority-owned businesses. By facilitating greater access to infrastructure and technology, this legislation played a role in leveling the playing field, albeit within an industry that would soon evolve far beyond its original scope.

While these initiatives undeniably moved the needle, their efficacy in the face of rapid technological advancement, particularly in the AI sector, remains a subject of ongoing debate. The complex landscape of today's tech industry calls for policies that are not only reactive to past inequalities but also proactive in anticipating the challenges faced by minority communities. The rapid advancement of AI has highlighted both new opportunities and emerging disparities, requiring a comprehensive approach to policy formulation that emphasizes both equity and inclusivity.

Contemporary Policies and Their Impact

As artificial intelligence continues its exponential growth, policymakers have recognized the need to address the unique obstacles faced by minority-owned businesses within this transformative sector. Federal programs like Small Business Innovation Research (SBIR) and Small Business Technology Transfer (STTR) play a key role in this arena, offering funding to small businesses, including those owned by African Americans, for research and development initiatives with commercialization potential. These programs serve as a bridge, helping small minority-led enterprises advance from conceptual ideas to fully realized, marketable technologies. By providing crucial financial support, these initiatives help African American entrepreneurs break into high-stakes industries where capital investment is essential to competing effectively.

Additionally, the Minority Business Development Agency (MBDA) of the US Department of Commerce has been instrumental in promoting the growth of minority-owned tech firms, including those focused on AI. The MBDA's mission is to foster the growth of minority-owned businesses, enhance their competitive standing, and facilitate entry into emerging sectors like AI. This agency offers a lifeline of support – through counseling, funding resources, and business development assistance – that enables minority entrepreneurs to overcome structural barriers and build sustainable enterprises.

State-level initiatives also play a vital role. Many states have introduced their own programs to foster minority entrepreneurship through targeted grants, preferential contracting policies, and better access to capital. Programs aimed at boosting minority participation in technology sectors, such as innovation hubs and business incubators, have made a notable impact by reducing some of the systemic challenges African American entrepreneurs face in accessing resources. These efforts, while beneficial, must be scaled and consistently maintained to ensure that minority businesses have long-term support and access to growth opportunities.

However, despite the existence of these initiatives, significant hurdles remain. Minority-owned businesses continue to face challenges in accessing capital, often due to systemic biases in lending practices. African American entrepreneurs are still disproportionately denied access to the funding they need, hindering their ability to scale their operations or engage in the research and development necessary for the AI sector. Furthermore, navigating the regulatory landscape and competing for government contracts present additional obstacles, particularly for smaller firms lacking the resources of larger competitors. The bureaucratic complexities of securing federal contracts are often compounded by a lack of familiarity with the intricate requirements involved, placing minority-owned firms at a disadvantage.

The Need for Inclusive AI Policies

The role of inclusive policy is central to shaping who benefits from advancements in artificial intelligence. Historically, African American entrepreneurs have been excluded from the full benefits of policy initiatives due to systemic biases and their limited presence in decision-making circles. In the AI sector, inclusive policies can bridge crucial gaps in funding, technology, and education, enabling entrepreneurs from marginalized communities to engage meaningfully in innovation. Without intervention, the development of AI risks reflecting and perpetuating the biases of those who predominantly shape its trajectory.

Initiatives like tax incentives for minority-owned AI firms and grants prioritizing underrepresented founders are practical starting points for addressing inequality. These financial incentives help provide a safety net for minority-owned businesses, giving them the room to innovate without the constant pressure of immediate profitability. Moreover, policies mandating diverse representation on AI development teams can help ensure that the resulting technologies reflect the needs of a broader spectrum of society, not just the privileged few. Inclusivity in AI development is not just a matter of justice; it is a prerequisite for robust, socially responsible innovation that has the potential to benefit all communities. If AI is to fulfill its promise of creating transformative solutions, it must be inclusive by design, accounting for a wide variety of perspectives and experiences.

Accountability in AI Development and Its Impact

As AI systems become increasingly embedded in our daily lives, the need for accountability in their development intensifies. Many African American entrepreneurs face disadvantages not only due to limited access to capital but also because they often suffer from biases perpetuated by AI systems. From hiring algorithms that systematically disadvantage Black candidates to credit scoring models that fail to adequately serve minority communities, flawed AI systems represent a growing challenge. The biases inherent in these systems are frequently the result of the data they are trained on, which may lack diversity or reinforce societal prejudices.

A robust regulatory framework that ensures developers are held accountable for the fairness, transparency, and accuracy of their AI systems is crucial. African American entrepreneurs have an important role to play in advocating for these frameworks, using their experiences to push for diverse datasets, transparent algorithms, and anti-bias measures, ultimately contributing to a fairer technology landscape. These advocacy efforts can also extend to pushing for greater collaboration between industry and academia to establish industry standards for ethical AI. Transparency in AI development must be woven into the regulatory fabric to ensure that these technologies serve all people equitably.

Empowering Communities Through Local Initiatives

Local policies also have a critical role in empowering African American entrepreneurs. Cities like Atlanta and Detroit, which have rich legacies of African American entrepreneurship, offer examples of how local governments can create inclusive tech ecosystems that foster AI innovation. Municipal programs investing in tech hubs, small business grants, and digital literacy initiatives create opportunities for grassroots innovation that can directly benefit the community. These cities have the potential to become models for inclusive technology growth by ensuring that minority entrepreneurs have access to the necessary infrastructure, networks, and funding to succeed in the AI sector.

Collaborations between local governments and historically Black colleges and universities (HBCUs) can amplify these efforts by offering training programs, mentorship opportunities, and access to resources for budding entrepreneurs. Such initiatives help bridge the skills gap while building resilient communities poised to participate fully in the AI economy. By investing in education and entrepreneurship programs at HBCUs, local governments not only uplift individual students and entrepreneurs but also create a multiplier effect that benefits entire communities.

The Importance of Representation in Policy Development

A significant barrier to overcoming inequity is the lack of African American representation in policy development. The absence of minority voices in the committees, boards, and working groups responsible for shaping technology policy means that policies often fail to account for the unique barriers faced by African American entrepreneurs; or worse, inadvertently reinforce them. Ensuring these voices are present is paramount for crafting policies that genuinely support inclusive growth.

Addressing this requires deliberate action. Establishing advisory councils focused specifically on minority participation in AI and tech policy, creating fellowships to train African American professionals for roles in policymaking, and partnering with advocacy organizations to amplify Black voices are just some of the ways representation can be improved. Greater representation ensures that the concerns of minority communities are not only heard but also inform the policies that shape the technology landscape. Such measures will pave the way for policies that understand and address the systemic challenges faced by African American entrepreneurs, providing a more equitable foundation for progress.

Lessons From the Global Policy Landscape

The challenges faced by African American entrepreneurs are not unique; marginalized communities across the globe confront similar struggles regarding access and representation in technology. Examining global policies can provide valuable lessons for driving equity in AI. For example, the European Union's General Data Protection Regulation (GDPR) has set high standards for data privacy, promoting accountability and transparency, principles that are vital for preventing the misuse of community data and ensuring ethical AI practices. These regulations have forced companies to take data protection seriously, offering a framework that US policymakers can learn from, especially in ensuring that minority communities are not exploited or marginalized by the development and deployment of AI technologies.

In countries like Rwanda, government investment in AI and technology education has successfully sparked entrepreneurship and innovation. Such examples demonstrate the transformative power of targeted government intervention and highlight the importance of creating inclusive policy frameworks in the US that are proactive rather than reactive. The Rwandan government's initiatives serve as a blueprint for how strategic investment in technology infrastructure and education can transform a community, providing a stark reminder of what is possible when inclusivity is placed at the core of policy design.

Public–Private Partnerships and Their Role in Innovation

The realization of effective policies often requires robust collaboration between public institutions and the private sector. Public–private partnerships offer an opportunity to bridge gaps in funding, expertise, and mentorship. Corporations can play a significant role in providing resources for minority-led startups, partnering with local governments to develop training initiatives, and contributing to the creation of an inclusive AI ecosystem. These partnerships can offer pathways for African American entrepreneurs that might otherwise be inaccessible, helping to create a more balanced technology landscape.

These partnerships can take numerous forms: for example, an AI company collaborating with a local municipality to provide free coding boot camps for underserved communities. Such efforts can offer African American entrepreneurs the skills and networks needed to succeed in the AI economy, further demonstrating that inclusive innovation requires contributions from all sectors of society. Moreover, these partnerships can accelerate the integration of emerging technologies into public infrastructure, fostering an environment of innovation that benefits everyone while ensuring minority voices are included in these transformative efforts.

Addressing Barriers in Government Procurement

Government procurement represents a substantial opportunity for African American entrepreneurs, particularly within the AI sector. Yet, securing government contracts remains challenging due to complex application processes, opaque selection criteria, and inherent biases. Reforming these procurement policies is crucial for providing equitable access. Government contracts can be game changers for small businesses, offering stable income streams that enable further growth and investment in innovation.

This could include setting aside contracts specifically for minority-led AI startups, simplifying the application process, and offering technical assistance to help minority businesses compete effectively. Additionally, transparency in procurement processes is essential to ensuring that African American entrepreneurs have a fair shot at securing contracts. Such measures would not only help scale minority-owned businesses but would also ensure that public sector projects benefit from the unique perspectives of a diverse set of innovators. Procurement reform, when done right, can act as a powerful equalizer, providing opportunities that promote sustained growth and innovation in underrepresented communities.

Future-Oriented Policies: Anticipating New Challenges

AI is evolving rapidly, and policies must evolve with it to ensure inclusivity and fairness. African American entrepreneurs have an opportunity to help shape the frameworks governing emerging technologies such as quantum computing and neural interfaces, areas that could present even greater challenges if inclusivity is not prioritized from the start. The rapid pace of technological development means that forward-thinking policies must be in place to guide equitable participation from the outset.

Policies should proactively encourage underrepresented groups to participate in research and development in these areas. This means not only setting standards for ethical development but also providing targeted funding and support to entrepreneurs, so they are positioned not only as participants but as leaders in these burgeoning fields. Proactive policies can be instrumental in building diverse ecosystems of innovation that ensure marginalized voices are represented in both the development and the governance of new technologies.

A Call to Collective Action

The intersection of policy and technological progress is where the future of African American entrepreneurship in AI will be defined. Ensuring equitable access to resources, representation in policymaking, and accountability in AI development will require sustained, collective action. Policymakers, advocacy groups, and entrepreneurs must collaborate to create a future where innovation is inclusive, and the benefits of AI are shared widely.

African American entrepreneurs are uniquely positioned to drive this change by using their platforms to advocate for policies that reflect their experiences and values. By shaping today's policies, they lay the groundwork for a more equitable and prosperous future – not only for themselves but for future generations of innovators. Advocacy, mentorship, and direct involvement in policy discussions are essential tools that can be wielded to ensure AI evolves in a way that benefits everyone, not just a privileged few.

Implementation Challenges and Policy Recommendations

While many policies aimed at supporting minority entrepreneurs are well-intentioned, their impact is often muted by obstacles in implementation. Entrepreneurs may not be fully aware of available programs due to insufficient outreach, while bureaucratic processes and complex eligibility criteria can deter participation. Inadequate funding and a lack of accountability mechanisms also limit the effectiveness of many initiatives. These challenges highlight the importance of a holistic approach to policy implementation, one that considers not only the availability of resources but also the accessibility and transparency of those resources.

Addressing these challenges requires several key steps. First, increased funding must be allocated to programs that support minority-owned businesses in AI, including grants for R&D and accelerator programs. Streamlining bureaucratic processes is also essential to make these resources accessible. Reducing the complexity of application requirements and expediting approval processes can make a significant difference for smaller firms with fewer administrative resources. Enhanced outreach strategies must be employed to ensure awareness of available support, particularly within underrepresented communities. Outreach should include partnerships with local organizations and digital platforms that are accessible to all entrepreneurs.

Furthermore, data collection and analysis are crucial for understanding the real-world impact of these policies and identifying areas for improvement. Data-driven insights can inform future policy adjustments, making initiatives more effective and better tailored to the needs of African American entrepreneurs. Collaboration between government agencies, private corporations, and community organizations can also create a supportive ecosystem where African American entrepreneurs can thrive. Public–private collaborations that focus on skill-building, networking, and funding are especially important in the AI sector, where technical expertise and early funding can make or break an initiative.

By addressing these obstacles, we can unlock the full potential of African American entrepreneurship in AI, driving innovation and economic growth for all. A focused commitment to inclusivity, education, and systemic reform is essential to ensuring that the AI revolution benefits not just a select few, but everyone. Only by recognizing the unique challenges and implementing forward-thinking, effective policies can we ensure that African American entrepreneurs have the opportunity to lead, innovate, and shape the future of AI. These collective efforts will ultimately drive a more vibrant, diverse, and resilient technological landscape that serves all of humanity.

Inspiration Bite: Chinasa T. Okolo

Chinasa T. Okolo is a Nigerian-American computer scientist and researcher whose work centers on the ethical implications of AI technologies, particularly in relation to marginalized communities. As a fellow at the Brookings Institution, she contributes to policy discussions on AI's impact on the Global South, advocating for inclusive and equitable technological development. Okolo's research emphasizes the importance of considering diverse perspectives in AI policy-making to ensure that technological advancements benefit all segments of society.

Source: https://awiu.org/bio/chinasa-t-okolo-ph-d/

Reflection Prompts

What policies or regulations have directly impacted your ability to succeed as an entrepreneur? How have you adapted?

How can you advocate for policies that support equitable access to technology and funding in the African American community?

What would you include in a policy agenda to help underrepresented entrepreneurs thrive in the AI era?

Chapter 7

Funding the Future

> The great economic equalizer of our generation, the revolution of this generation, is indeed technology. And by embedding these skills and abilities in our youth today, we can change the nation – one girl, one woman and one generation at a time. – Kimberly Bryant, founder of Black Girls Code.

Securing funding is often the most crucial step in transforming a promising idea into a thriving business. For African American entrepreneurs in the Artificial Intelligence (AI) sector, navigating the investment landscape presents unique challenges. These challenges stem from systemic barriers, limited access to networks, and the complexities of the investment ecosystem. This chapter explores the intricacies of funding AI ventures, exploring available capital sources, the obstacles minority entrepreneurs face, and strategies to overcome these financial hurdles to build successful AI businesses. The aim is not only to provide practical guidance but also to inspire resilience and ambition among African American founders striving to make their mark in the AI industry.

AI VentureSphere: Funding the Future

Recognizing that lack of funding was the primary barrier preventing African American entrepreneurs from scaling their ventures, Angela Reeves launched AI VentureSphere, an AI-driven funding platform. By analyzing historical funding patterns, market viability, and founder potential, the platform provided a fair and unbiased assessment of which ventures were most likely to succeed. Angela's AI model was trained to disregard factors like racial bias, focusing instead on the core strengths of the business ideas and their potential impact. By creating a more inclusive funding ecosystem, AI VentureSphere opened doors for entrepreneurs who were traditionally overlooked by mainstream investors. In addition to funding, the platform also matched entrepreneurs with strategic advisors, creating a holistic support system that increased their chances of long-term success. Angela's innovation showed that AI could disrupt not just markets but also the very systems of inequality that had constrained opportunities for far too long.

AI Empowered, 71–82

Published under exclusive licence by Emerald Publishing Limited
doi:10.1108/978-1-83662-816-320251008

Understanding the Investment Ecosystem

The investment ecosystem for AI startups is a complex and dynamic network that includes diverse players, each with unique motivations, expectations, and investment approaches. These players include venture capital firms, angel investors, corporate venture capital (CVC), government funding agencies, accelerators, incubators, and crowdfunding platforms. Understanding the nuances of each source is critical for AI entrepreneurs seeking to navigate the landscape effectively.

Venture capital firms pool funds from multiple sources to invest in high-growth startups with significant return potential. Many of these firms have dedicated partners focusing exclusively on AI, recognizing the transformative power of this technology. Venture capital provides large amounts of capital, which is often essential for scaling AI solutions that require substantial computing power, data acquisition, and top-tier technical talent. However, venture capital funding often comes with the expectation of high returns, leading to pressure for rapid growth.

Angel investors, on the other hand, are high-net-worth individuals who invest in early-stage startups and often provide mentorship alongside financial support. This combination of financial backing and expertise can be invaluable for startups navigating the uncertainties of their initial phases. Angels are typically more willing to take risks on unproven ideas, especially when the founding team has strong potential and a compelling vision.

CVC offers funding through dedicated investment arms of large corporations, providing not only capital but also strategic resources and expertise. Corporations like Google, Microsoft, and Amazon have recognized the value of AI in shaping future industries and have invested heavily in promising startups. CVC investments often come with opportunities for partnership, access to proprietary datasets, and integration with existing technological ecosystems. Such benefits can be instrumental for AI startups seeking not only funding but also the strategic alliances needed for large-scale deployment.

Government funding agencies are an important part of the investment landscape, offering grants and contracts to support AI research, especially in areas of social good or national interest. For instance, agencies such as the National Science Foundation (NSF) and the Defense Advanced Research Projects Agency (DARPA) provide significant funding opportunities for AI projects that align with their missions. These grants can be particularly beneficial for minority entrepreneurs focused on research and development, as they do not require equity exchange, thereby allowing founders to maintain ownership of their companies.

Accelerators and incubators further aid startups by providing mentorship, workspace, and seed funding, helping them build momentum during critical early stages. Programs like Y Combinator and Techstars offer valuable resources that go beyond mere financial support; they provide networking opportunities, access to potential investors, and a collaborative environment conducive to rapid development. African American entrepreneurs, in particular, can benefit from specialized accelerators such as the Minority Business Accelerator, which is tailored to address the unique challenges faced by minority founders.

Lastly, crowdfunding platforms have democratized funding, allowing entrepreneurs to connect directly with the public to raise capital for their projects. Platforms like Kickstarter, GoFundMe, and Indiegogo enable founders to showcase their visions and gain community support. Crowd funding not only raises capital but also validates ideas, as it allows entrepreneurs to gauge public interest and build a loyal customer base before launching their products.

Trends Shaping AI Investment

The landscape of AI investment is constantly evolving, with emerging trends reshaping the flow of capital. Investors are becoming increasingly specialized, focusing on particular AI applications, technologies, or industries. This specialization reflects a deeper understanding of the different ways AI can be applied, from healthcare and education to logistics and finance. Investors with industry-specific knowledge can add considerable value to startups by providing domain expertise and valuable industry contacts.

Ethical AI is gaining significant attention, with investors prioritizing startups that address societal challenges responsibly. There is a growing awareness of the potential for AI technologies to perpetuate biases and create ethical dilemmas, leading to an emphasis on solutions that actively mitigate these risks. Investors are increasingly attracted to startups that demonstrate a commitment to transparency, fairness, and ethical governance. This trend represents an opportunity for African American entrepreneurs who often have unique insights into the biases embedded within AI algorithms and can develop solutions to address these issues.

There is also a shift toward funding AI solutions that have practical, real-world applications, demonstrate market traction, and have a clear pathway to monetization. Investors are more inclined to support projects that solve pressing problems, generate immediate value, and show evidence of customer adoption. As AI technologies become more integrated into daily life, investors are less interested in abstract ideas and more focused on tangible outcomes that can disrupt existing industries or create new markets.

The growth of AI-focused funds further highlights the appetite for investment in this space. Funds such as the AI Fund, led by prominent industry figures, are dedicated to nurturing AI startups through targeted investments. Importantly, there is growing recognition of the value of diverse perspectives in AI development. This trend has led to more initiatives specifically focused on funding underrepresented entrepreneurs, including African American founders. Diversity in AI development is seen as essential for ensuring that AI solutions benefit all communities and do not inadvertently exacerbate existing inequalities.

Sources of Capital: Traditional and Alternative Routes

AI entrepreneurs have access to various funding routes, each with its own set of advantages and limitations. These routes can be categorized as either traditional or alternative funding sources. Each source comes with its own set of challenges, rewards, and expectations, and understanding these differences is crucial for entrepreneurs to make informed decisions.

Traditional funding routes include venture capital and angel investments. Venture capital can provide substantial growth capital but comes with expectations for equity and rapid scaling. The pressure from venture capital investors to achieve quick growth and high returns can be a double-edged sword, pushing startups to scale prematurely or take risks that may not align with their long-term vision. Nevertheless, for AI companies with a scalable product and a large addressable market, venture capital can be instrumental in achieving market dominance.

Angel investors may offer smaller amounts of funding, but they often accompany their investment with valuable mentorship. Many angels have previously been successful entrepreneurs themselves and understand the challenges inherent in building a business from scratch. This makes angel investors particularly valuable to startups in their earliest stages, where guidance can sometimes be even more crucial than capital.

Bank loans are another traditional source of funding, though they may be difficult to secure for early-stage AI startups due to stringent requirements and a lack of collateral. Banks are generally more risk-averse compared to other investors, which means that AI startups, particularly those focused on speculative or research-driven projects, may struggle to meet the qualifications needed for loans. However, for more established startups with a proven track record, bank loans can be a viable option for obtaining additional working capital without giving up equity.

Alternative funding options offer flexible approaches that can be particularly beneficial for minority entrepreneurs. Crowd funding allows startups to raise smaller amounts of capital by building community support through compelling marketing campaigns. Crowdfunding success requires a strong narrative, and African American founders have the opportunity to connect with audiences on a personal level, sharing not only their business ideas but also their personal journeys, challenges, and aspirations. This kind of storytelling can attract backers who are motivated by more than just financial returns: they want to see the entrepreneurs succeed.

Revenue-based financing, which involves sharing a portion of future revenues with investors, is less dilutive compared to equity financing and allows founders to retain control. This model is attractive for startups with predictable revenue streams, as repayment scales with the company's earnings, providing flexibility during both growth and downturn periods. This is an advantageous funding route for AI startups offering subscription-based services or SaaS products, where revenue streams are steady and predictable.

Government grants and nonprofit foundation funding are also important, providing nondilutive capital to help entrepreneurs bring innovative ideas to market. Programs like the Small Business Innovation Research (SBIR) and Small Business Technology Transfer (STTR) offer grants aimed at early-stage technology development. These funds can be instrumental in the research and prototyping phases, which are crucial in AI ventures that require substantial technical development before becoming commercially viable. Nonprofits also provide funding and mentorship programs that focus on community impact, which can be a natural fit for African American entrepreneurs aiming to develop socially conscious AI solutions.

Lastly, accelerators and incubators can provide seed funding, mentorship, and valuable industry connections. The combination of funding, mentorship, and structured growth programs accelerators provide helps startups overcome many of the hurdles typically encountered in the early stages. Programs like AI NexusLab and Element AI, which are dedicated to AI startups, offer specific expertise and access to an AI-centric network, making them highly relevant for entrepreneurs looking to develop cutting-edge technologies.

Venture Capital and Angel Investors in the AI Space

Venture capital and angel investors play a pivotal role in the AI startup ecosystem, particularly because of the unique demands of building AI technologies, which often require substantial early-stage capital for research, data acquisition, and model training. Many venture capital firms specialize in AI investments, and large technology companies like Google, Microsoft, and IBM often invest through their corporate venture arms. Such investments not only offer financial support but also strategic advantages, such as access to cutting-edge infrastructure, technical expertise, and distribution networks.

Networks like Black Angel Tech Fund specifically target supporting Black entrepreneurs in tech, creating pathways for growth that might not exist in traditional venture capital circles. The creation of funds dedicated to minority entrepreneurs helps address the long-standing funding disparities, providing African American founders with access to investors who understand their unique challenges and are committed to their success.

AI investors generally prioritize startups that demonstrate strong teams with proven technical expertise, unique technologies with competitive advantages, significant market opportunities, and evidence of market traction. Investors look for founders who have deep domain knowledge and the ability to execute on their vision. For African American entrepreneurs, building a strong team with complementary skills and a solid track record in AI development can significantly boost investor confidence.

Intellectual property protection, such as patents or trade secrets, further enhances a startup's value proposition to investors. Startups with patented technologies are particularly attractive to venture capitalists, as IP serves as a barrier to entry for competitors and provides a basis for long-term value creation. Establishing these factors can significantly increase an AI startup's appeal to venture capitalists and angel investors, making it easier to secure substantial funding for scaling operations.

The Capital Divide: Systemic Barriers in Funding

Access to capital remains one of the most significant hurdles for African American entrepreneurs, particularly in high-tech industries like AI. Systemic racism has historically constrained Black entrepreneurs' ability to secure funding through traditional channels, such as bank loans and venture capital. Research indicates that African American startups receive only a small fraction (approximately 1%) of venture capital investments, a disparity that reflects deep-rooted biases in the investment community.

This disparity is rooted in several factors, including a lack of representation among decision-makers at investment firms, implicit biases, and assumptions about market potential that often exclude innovations emerging from underrepresented communities. Most venture capitalists are white and male, and this homogeneity can lead to a lack of understanding or appreciation for the market needs addressed by minority entrepreneurs. As a result, African American founders often face skepticism that their counterparts do not, regardless of the potential of their technology or the quality of their business model.

Overcoming these challenges requires systemic change within the investment community, including increasing diversity among decision-makers and implementing initiatives that actively support minority entrepreneurs. Some venture capital firms are beginning to recognize the importance of diversity, not just as a moral imperative but as a business opportunity. Diverse teams are more likely to identify unique market opportunities and innovate in ways that homogenous teams might not. As such, creating a more inclusive investment ecosystem is not only beneficial for minority entrepreneurs but also advantageous for investors seeking innovative and disruptive technologies.

Crowdfunding as a Democratized Funding Source

Crowdfunding has become a powerful funding source for African American entrepreneurs, offering an opportunity to raise capital without relying on traditional financial institutions. Platforms like Kickstarter, GoFundMe, and Indiegogo allow entrepreneurs to present their ideas directly to the public, which can generate both funding and community support. Crowdfunding is particularly impactful for African American entrepreneurs, who may find it challenging to gain traction with traditional investors due to systemic biases.

For African American entrepreneurs in AI, crowdfunding can serve as both a fundraising and marketing tool. These platforms allow founders to tell their stories authentically, connecting with backers who are motivated by the desire to support underrepresented voices in tech. Crowdfunding campaigns can be highly effective when entrepreneurs wield social networks, storytelling, and visuals to convey the significance of their work. Successful campaigns not only generate the capital needed to launch or grow a business but also create a base of early adopters and brand advocates who contribute to long-term success.

By leveraging storytelling and social networks, entrepreneurs can bypass traditional gatekeepers and bring their ideas to life. Crowd funding also serves as a market validation tool: successful campaigns signal that there is demand for a product, making it easier to attract follow-on investments from venture capital or angel investors. For African American entrepreneurs, this combination of funding, marketing, and validation can be transformative, providing the momentum needed to overcome systemic barriers.

Innovative Approaches to Venture Capital

To address systemic barriers within the traditional venture capital model, new approaches have emerged. Funds like the New Voices Fund and Black Angel Tech Fund are designed to support minority founders, helping bridge the gap in access to capital. These funds focus on leveling the playing field for underrepresented entrepreneurs by providing not only financial backing but also mentorship, industry connections, and strategic guidance that are crucial for growth.

African American entrepreneurs can also benefit from joining accelerators and incubators that prioritize diversity, participating in pitch competitions that focus on inclusion, and networking with angel investors who have an interest in untapped markets. Such programs not only provide financial resources but also help entrepreneurs gain visibility and credibility in the industry. Pitch competitions like Startup Runway and events like Black Women Talk Tech offer platforms for minority founders to showcase their innovations and gain critical exposure to investors actively seeking to diversify their portfolios.

These innovative approaches not only increase access to funding but also connect entrepreneurs with mentors and industry resources to foster long-term growth. By seeking culturally aligned investors and supportive communities, minority entrepreneurs can find opportunities that better match their unique needs. Culturally aligned investors are more likely to understand the challenges minority entrepreneurs face and are therefore better positioned to offer support beyond mere financial investment. This support can be instrumental in navigating the often-turbulent waters of startup growth and scaling.

Nontraditional Funding Models: Revenue-Based Financing (RBF)

RBF presents a flexible alternative to traditional loans and equity financing. Under this model, investors provide upfront capital in exchange for a percentage of future revenues. This approach aligns investor interests with the success of the business, making it particularly appealing for African American entrepreneurs who wish to avoid equity dilution. By tying repayment to revenue, RBF mitigates the risks associated with fixed loan payments, especially for startups that may experience fluctuating cash flows.

RBF works well for AI businesses with predictable revenue streams, such as subscription-based models or Software as a Service (SaaS) platforms. This type of financing is gaining traction as more startups seek alternatives that allow them to retain control of their companies. For African American entrepreneurs, RBF is an attractive option because it ensures founders can maintain majority ownership while still accessing the capital needed for growth. This model is especially relevant in the AI sector, where growth often depends on scaling infrastructure and hiring skilled talent, both of which require significant investment.

By considering nontraditional funding models like RBF, African American entrepreneurs can access the financial resources they need without compromising ownership or control of their companies. Maintaining control is particularly important for minority founders, as it allows them to preserve their vision and ensure that their products reflect their values and serve their communities effectively.

Harnessing Government and Nonprofit Grants

Government agencies and nonprofit organizations offer valuable funding opportunities for minority entrepreneurs in AI. Programs like the Small Business Innovation Research (SBIR) and Small Business Technology Transfer (STTR) provide grants that can be instrumental in the research and development phases of AI ventures. These grants are particularly advantageous because they are nondilutive, meaning they do not require the entrepreneur to give up equity, allowing founders to maintain control over their businesses.

Nonprofits like Black Founders and Code2040 also offer funding, mentorship, and support tailored to African American entrepreneurs, often focusing on community impact. These organizations recognize the systemic barriers faced by minority entrepreneurs and aim to empower them by providing resources that are often inaccessible through traditional channels. Funding from nonprofits is often accompanied by mentorship and strategic guidance, which can help founders refine their business models and prepare for future funding rounds.

Although the application process for these grants can be demanding, requiring detailed proposals and measurable outcomes, the nondilutive nature of these funds makes them an invaluable resource for growth. Entrepreneurs seeking to scale their AI ventures without sacrificing ownership can greatly benefit from such opportunities. Government and nonprofit grants are particularly useful for funding the early stages of product development, enabling startups to reach milestones that make them more attractive to private investors later on.

The Role of Financial Literacy in Securing Funding

Financial literacy is crucial for successful entrepreneurship, yet many African American founders lack access to essential financial education. Understanding key financial concepts such as equity dilution, interest rates, and cash flow management is critical for making informed funding decisions. A lack of financial literacy can lead to unfavorable deals that dilute ownership unnecessarily or result in untenable debt obligations.

African American entrepreneurs can enhance their financial literacy through workshops, online courses, and mentorship programs offered by organizations like the National Minority Supplier Development Council (NMSDC) and

Operation HOPE. By developing a solid understanding of financial principles, entrepreneurs can approach funding opportunities with greater confidence and clarity. Financial literacy also helps founders in negotiating with investors, understanding the implications of term sheets, and planning for long-term financial health.

A solid foundation in financial literacy is also essential for effective cash flow management. AI startups, in particular, often require significant initial investments before revenue generation becomes consistent. Being able to forecast cash flow needs, manage operating expenses, and allocate resources effectively can make the difference between success and failure. For African American entrepreneurs, who may have less access to emergency funding from personal networks, strong financial planning is even more critical.

Building Funding Networks: The Power of Relationships

In the investment world, relationships are often as important as financial metrics. African American entrepreneurs can expand their access to capital by actively cultivating relationships with investors, mentors, and peers. These relationships not only provide access to funding but also offer valuable guidance, mentorship, and strategic connections that can accelerate growth.

Attending industry conferences, joining professional organizations, and participating in networking events are effective ways to build these connections. Conferences such as AfroTech and Black in AI provide platforms for African American entrepreneurs to connect with potential investors and collaborators, fostering authentic relationships that can lead to funding opportunities. By participating in such events, entrepreneurs can increase their visibility, pitch their ideas to a receptive audience, and form connections that may prove invaluable during their funding journey.

Mentorship is another crucial aspect of building a funding network. Mentors with experience in the tech industry can help African American founders navigate the complexities of startup growth, refine their business models, and connect with investors. Initiatives like Founder Gym and Venture Noire focus specifically on equipping minority entrepreneurs with the skills, knowledge, and connections they need to succeed. By fostering genuine, long-term relationships, entrepreneurs can build trust and gain advocates who champion their ideas within funding circles.

Success Stories: Breaking Through the Funding Barrier

Success stories of African American entrepreneurs who have secured funding provide both inspiration and valuable lessons. These examples demonstrate that, despite the barriers, it is possible to overcome obstacles and achieve success in the AI space. For example, Kimberly Bryant, founder of Black Girls Code, has successfully raised millions through a mix of crowdfunding, corporate sponsorships, and grants to empower young Black girls to pursue careers in tech. Her success highlights the importance of community-driven support and the impact of aligning business goals with broader social missions.

Similarly, Jewel Burks Solomon, co-founder of Partpic, secured venture capital to scale her AI-powered parts recognition platform, which was eventually acquired by Amazon. Her journey underscores the importance of building a strong team, securing early traction, and maintaining a clear focus on solving a real-world problem. These stories highlight the power of persistence, creativity, and community support in overcoming funding challenges. They serve as proof that African American entrepreneurs can not only compete in the tech industry but can also lead the way in AI innovation.

By learning from these examples, African American entrepreneurs can draw insights and inspiration for navigating their own funding journeys. These success stories also help to change the narrative around African American entrepreneurship in tech, proving that diversity is not a barrier to innovation but rather a strength that leads to more inclusive and effective solutions.

A Vision for Inclusive Investment

Achieving equity in funding requires systemic change. Venture capital firms, government agencies, and private investors must prioritize diversity in their funding portfolios by setting aside capital for minority-led ventures, creating mentorship programs, and addressing biases in the funding process. Many firms are now recognizing the value of diversity, not only from a social responsibility standpoint but also from a profitability perspective, as diverse teams are more likely to innovate and capture overlooked markets.

African American entrepreneurs also play a critical role in this vision by advocating for inclusive investment practices and supporting peer ventures. By forming networks and advocating for each other, minority entrepreneurs can help build a community that amplifies their collective voice. Collaborative efforts, such as syndicate investing among Black angel investors, can provide a way to pool resources and invest in promising minority-led startups.

Together, these efforts can create a more equitable funding ecosystem and ensure that the future of AI entrepreneurship reflects the diversity and creativity of all communities. It is essential for investors, policymakers, and entrepreneurs to work together to dismantle the systemic barriers that have historically limited opportunities for African American founders. By creating an environment that encourages diverse perspectives, the AI industry can build technologies that benefit society as a whole.

Challenges and Strategies for African American Entrepreneurs

African American entrepreneurs in the AI space often face additional challenges related to bias, limited networks, and a lack of track record. Implicit biases and underrepresentation in the investment community can create barriers, while limited access to influential networks may restrict opportunities to get in front of potential investors. Additionally, many Black entrepreneurs may be first-time founders, which makes securing funding from traditional sources more difficult.

To overcome these challenges, African American entrepreneurs should focus on building strong networks, leveraging supportive programs, crafting compelling pitches, and demonstrating early traction through pilot projects and proof-of-concept initiatives. Participating in specialized accelerators that cater to minority entrepreneurs, such as Backstage Capital Accelerator, can provide critical support and resources that make the difference in gaining investor attention. These programs not only provide funding but also prepare founders for the rigorous demands of scaling their startups.

Exploring alternative funding sources – such as crowdfunding, grants, and revenue-based financing – can also help provide the necessary capital. Crowdfunding platforms, in particular, offer an opportunity to tell a compelling personal story and build a loyal community of early adopters. Demonstrating traction through metrics such as user growth, revenue, or partnerships can also increase credibility and attract investor attention, helping entrepreneurs bridge the gap to larger funding rounds.

In addition, crafting a compelling pitch that highlights the unique value proposition of the AI solution, the problem it addresses, and the team's qualifications is essential. Investors need to understand not only the technology but also the market potential and the capability of the team to execute the vision. African American entrepreneurs can benefit from pitch workshops and mentoring programs that help them refine their messaging, anticipate investor questions, and present their ideas with confidence.

Securing funding is an essential milestone in the entrepreneurial journey, especially for African American entrepreneurs in the AI sector. By understanding the investment ecosystem, exploring diverse funding sources, building strong networks, and enhancing financial literacy, these entrepreneurs can navigate the complexities of the investment landscape and secure the capital needed to transform their innovative AI ideas into successful businesses. With persistence, creativity, and support from inclusive initiatives, they can overcome obstacles and help shape a more diverse and equitable AI industry.

The path forward requires systemic change and individual resilience. Investors must recognize the untapped potential within diverse communities, and African American entrepreneurs must continue to advocate for their place at the table, leveraging every available resource to bring their visions to life. Together, these efforts can ensure that AI, as a transformative technology, serves the needs and reflects the contributions of all people, creating a future that is not only technologically advanced but also equitable and inclusive.

Inspiration Bite: Iman Abuzeid

Dr. Iman Abuzeid is founder and CEO of Incredible Health, a digital platform that utilizes AI to streamline the hiring process for nurses in the United States. Under her leadership, Incredible Health has achieved a valuation exceeding $1 billion, making her one of the few Black female CEOs to reach such a milestone. Abuzeid's innovative approach addresses critical staffing shortages in healthcare by leveraging AI to match nurses with hospitals efficiently, thereby improving patient care and operational efficiency.

Source: https://www.forbes.com/profile/iman-abuzeid/

Reflection Prompts

What funding challenges have you faced in pursuing your goals? How did you overcome them, or what could have helped?

What steps can you take to make yourself or your business more attractive to investors or funding sources?

How can you use innovative funding strategies, such as crowdfunding or partnerships, to support your vision?

Chapter 8

Education and Empowerment

> Education is the most powerful weapon which you can use to change the world. – Nelson Mandela

In the rapidly evolving landscape of Artificial Intelligence (AI), education serves as the cornerstone for innovation and entrepreneurship. This chapter explores the critical role of education in empowering African American entrepreneurs to navigate the complexities of AI, develop cutting-edge solutions, and build successful businesses in this transformative field. By emphasizing access, inclusivity, and the cultivation of diverse skills, education becomes a powerful tool for dismantling systemic barriers and nurturing a new generation of African American AI leaders. This journey toward empowerment requires not only formal education but also community engagement, mentorship, and ongoing support that extend well beyond traditional academic settings.

AI Pathways: Education and Empowerment for All

Under the belief that education was the foundation of empowerment, Camille Johnson created AI Pathways, a platform designed to teach AI literacy to African American youth and aspiring entrepreneurs. AI Pathways used adaptive learning algorithms to personalize educational content, ensuring that learners could progress at their own pace while focusing on areas where they needed the most help. By partnering with historically Black colleges and universities (HBCUs), Camille provided access to specialized AI courses that focused on practical, real-world applications, including entrepreneurship. The platform gamified learning, making complex concepts accessible and engaging, even for those without a technical background. Camille's vision was to create a generation of AI-literate individuals who could participate in and shape the AI revolution, ensuring that African American voices were part of the technological future. AI Pathways empowered people to move from being passive consumers of technology to becoming its creators and innovators, driving progress in their communities.

AI Empowered, 83–90

Published under exclusive licence by Emerald Publishing Limited
doi:10.1108/978-1-83662-816-320251009

The Educational Imperative: Shaping AI Entrepreneurs

Education is not simply the acquisition of knowledge; it is the cultivation of skills, the fostering of critical thinking, and the empowerment of individuals to shape their own futures. In the context of AI entrepreneurship, education does far more than just teach the technical aspects of machine learning, data science, and related fields. It equips aspiring entrepreneurs with the ability to turn technological innovations into thriving businesses, emphasizing the importance of ethical considerations and critical thinking skills. For African American entrepreneurs, who often face systemic barriers and underrepresentation in the tech industry, quality education in AI can be a powerful equalizer, providing the knowledge and tools necessary to compete in a rapidly changing technological landscape.

Education in AI entrepreneurship is multifaceted: it involves imparting technical knowledge, nurturing business acumen, creating networking opportunities, and instilling a sense of ethical responsibility. These elements form the foundation for creating entrepreneurs who are capable of understanding AI technologies, innovating, and leading successful AI ventures. In a world increasingly driven by AI, educational opportunities must be accessible and tailored to empower underserved communities. The transformative potential of education lies in its capacity to break down barriers and inspire future leaders to drive meaningful change, bringing forth diverse perspectives and experiences that enrich the development of AI technologies.

To effectively support AI entrepreneurs, educational programs must address a wide range of needs. Technical training is essential, but equally important are lessons in leadership, ethics, and resilience. Entrepreneurs must learn how to build sustainable business models, collaborate with a diverse team, and tackle challenges creatively. By fostering an educational environment that encourages experimentation, collaboration, and a focus on societal impact, we can empower African American entrepreneurs to become not just participants, but leaders in the AI space.

The Importance of Early Exposure to AI Concepts

The journey toward AI literacy starts much earlier than higher education. For many African American students, a lack of early exposure to AI concepts in primary and secondary education creates a gap that can be challenging to bridge later in life. Introducing coding, robotics, and machine learning concepts at an early age is crucial for fostering curiosity and building foundational skills. Early education initiatives that bring AI to classrooms help demystify these technologies and empower students to imagine themselves as creators and innovators.

Programs like after-school coding clubs and summer camps specifically targeting underserved communities have shown promise in closing this gap. Organizations such as Black Girls Code provide firsthand experiences that make AI accessible and exciting for young learners. These initiatives not only spark interest in technology but also build confidence, demonstrating to students that they have a place in the AI revolution. This early exposure is vital in equipping African

American students with the skills and mindset necessary to pursue careers in AI entrepreneurship.

Early exposure to AI concepts has a ripple effect that extends beyond individual skill-building. It influences how students perceive themselves and their future opportunities. When young learners are introduced to the possibilities of AI and technology, they begin to envision futures that include roles as innovators, leaders, and creators. By cultivating an early interest in technology, we can inspire a new generation of African American leaders who feel empowered to drive AI for social good, business innovation, and community transformation.

HBCUs as Catalysts for AI Education

HBCUs have long been centers of excellence in African American education. In the era of AI, these institutions are uniquely positioned to bridge the skills gap by offering specialized programs that prepare students for leadership in the AI space. HBCUs, by establishing AI-focused research centers and forging partnerships with tech companies, can serve as powerful incubators for African American talent in technology and entrepreneurship.

Institutions like Howard University and Spelman College are already leading this effort, creating curricula that combine technical training with an emphasis on ethical AI and social impact. These initiatives ensure that students are not only learning to develop AI technologies but are also considering the ethical ramifications of their work, preparing them to be leaders in responsible AI innovation. By integrating technical rigor with social consciousness, HBCUs are cultivating a new generation of entrepreneurs who are ready to address systemic inequities through technology.

HBCUs also play a critical role in creating a sense of belonging for African American students in the tech space. In an industry where people of color are often underrepresented, HBCUs provide an inclusive environment that nurtures confidence, fosters community, and celebrates cultural identity. This supportive atmosphere is crucial for students who are embarking on the challenging journey of AI entrepreneurship. Through mentorship, alumni networks, and community engagement, HBCUs are not only educating students but also building ecosystems that empower graduates to thrive beyond the classroom.

AI Literacy for Nontechnical Entrepreneurs

AI entrepreneurship is not limited to those with a deep technical background. For African American entrepreneurs from nontechnical fields, gaining a foundational understanding of AI is crucial to leveraging its potential. Understanding how AI can be applied to enhance business operations, improve customer engagement, or create innovative products can significantly widen opportunities for entrepreneurship.

Workshops, online courses, and bootcamps tailored to nontechnical founders provide accessible entry points into the world of AI. These programs focus on practical applications, such as using AI tools for marketing, customer service, or logistics, empowering entrepreneurs to integrate AI into their business strategies without needing to become programmers. By making AI accessible to all, these initiatives help ensure that innovation is not limited to those with formal technical training.

Nontechnical entrepreneurs often bring fresh perspectives to AI development. By focusing on real-world problems and practical solutions, they can identify unique opportunities for AI that more technical practitioners might overlook. Encouraging AI literacy among nontechnical entrepreneurs helps diversify the range of AI applications, ensuring that the technology addresses a broad spectrum of needs and challenges. Moreover, this democratization of AI knowledge enables more voices to participate in shaping the future of technology, ultimately making AI more inclusive and responsive to community needs.

Closing the Resource Gap in AI Education

Access to quality AI education often depends on access to critical resources: modern computing equipment, high-speed internet, and experienced instructors. For many African American students, these resources remain out of reach, perpetuating the digital divide that hinders equitable participation in the tech industry. Addressing this disparity requires strategic community partnerships involving local governments, nonprofit organizations, and tech companies.

Providing laptops, coding software, and free internet access through community programs can significantly enhance the availability of AI education in underserved areas. Additionally, virtual learning platforms can bridge the gap, bringing top-tier AI education to students irrespective of their geographic location. By addressing these infrastructural barriers, it becomes possible to extend educational opportunities to all and nurture a diverse pool of future AI leaders.

Closing the resource gap is not only about providing physical tools but also about ensuring that quality instruction is available to students in every community. Initiatives that train educators, provide mentorship, and offer support networks can help level the playing field for African American students. By empowering teachers with the skills they need to effectively teach AI concepts, and by fostering environments where students feel supported and encouraged, we can create a system where everyone has the chance to succeed.

Mentorship as a Pillar of Empowerment

Mentorship is another crucial pillar in empowering African American entrepreneurs in the AI space. The guidance, insights, and opportunities provided by experienced mentors can make the difference between success and stagnation for early-stage entrepreneurs. Organizations like Black in AI and AI4ALL have created mentorship programs that connect African American students and entrepreneurs with seasoned professionals, fostering skill development and providing a sense of belonging in an industry where African Americans are often underrepresented.

Mentorship not only helps bridge the knowledge gap but also offers a support network that is instrumental in navigating the challenges of entrepreneurship. The relationships formed through these programs encourage perseverance and provide a pathway to opportunity, enabling aspiring entrepreneurs to overcome barriers and succeed in the AI field.

Effective mentorship goes beyond technical skills; it involves nurturing the personal growth and confidence of mentees. For many African American entrepreneurs, having a mentor who shares similar experiences and understands the unique challenges they face can be a powerful motivator. Mentors help mentees navigate systemic barriers, advocate for them in professional settings, and provide critical feedback that enhances both personal and professional development. By investing in mentorship programs, we invest in the resilience and success of future AI leaders.

Ethical AI Education: Teaching Responsibility Alongside Innovation

As AI becomes more pervasive, the need for ethical AI development grows. African American entrepreneurs, with their lived experiences of systemic bias, are uniquely positioned to create technologies that prioritize fairness and equity. Thus, education must go beyond the technical aspects of AI and emphasize its ethical implications. This includes considering how algorithms can perpetuate bias, understanding the importance of data privacy, and ensuring that AI technologies are used to empower communities rather than exploit them.

By embedding ethical considerations into AI curricula, educators can ensure that the next generation of African American entrepreneurs develops technologies that reflect their values and address societal challenges. This commitment to ethical innovation will be key to creating technologies that contribute positively to society and mitigate harm.

Ethical education also involves engaging with communities to understand the real-world impact of AI. Entrepreneurs must learn to ask critical questions: Who benefits from this technology? Who might be harmed? How can we ensure transparency and accountability? By teaching students to think deeply about these issues, we can foster a generation of AI leaders who are committed to using technology for social good. Ethical education helps ensure that AI solutions are not only innovative but also equitable and just.

Continuing Education in a Rapidly Evolving Field

The fast pace of AI innovation means that education cannot end with a degree. Learning lifelong is crucial for staying competitive and relevant in this dynamic field. African American entrepreneurs can benefit from ongoing training opportunities that keep them informed about the latest trends, tools, and techniques in AI.

Online platforms like Coursera, edX, and Udacity offer courses on advanced machine learning, natural language processing, and AI ethics, making it easier to continue learning. Attending industry conferences and participating in professional networks further ensures that entrepreneurs stay connected to the latest advancements in AI and maintain an active presence in the broader AI community.

Continuing education is not just about keeping up with technological advancements, it is also about expanding one's horizons and seeking inspiration from diverse fields. AI intersects with numerous disciplines, including healthcare, finance, art, and social sciences. By exploring these intersections, entrepreneurs can discover novel applications of AI and identify opportunities that are yet to be realized. Lifelong learning encourages adaptability and creativity, allowing entrepreneurs to remain at the forefront of innovation.

Community-Based Learning: Education Beyond the Classroom

Education does not happen exclusively within the four walls of a classroom. Community-based learning initiatives provide alternative avenues for African Americans to gain AI skills. Tech meetups, hackathons, and community workshops create environments where individuals can learn, collaborate, and innovate together.

Community centers equipped with AI tools and internet access can serve as hubs for firsthand learning and experimentation. These collaborative spaces allow entrepreneurs to evaluate ideas, receive feedback, and refine their skills in real-world scenarios, fostering a culture of practical learning and innovation.

Community-based learning also strengthens social bonds and builds networks of support that are crucial for entrepreneurship. Learning alongside peers who share similar challenges and aspirations creates a sense of solidarity and motivation. Hackathons, in particular, provide a unique opportunity to work on real problems, apply AI in creative ways, and gain exposure to the practical demands of technology development. These community-driven initiatives are instrumental in democratizing AI knowledge and fostering a culture of shared growth.

The Role of Storytelling in AI Education

Storytelling is an effective tool for demystifying AI and inspiring engagement. By highlighting the successes of African American entrepreneurs who have used AI to transform their businesses, educators can make AI more relatable and less intimidating. Case studies and narratives that showcase real-world applications of AI demonstrate its potential to solve problems and create opportunities. These stories can inspire others to explore AI entrepreneurship, serving as powerful reminders that the field is open to all who dare to innovate.

The stories of African American AI entrepreneurs serve as blueprints for success, illustrating the pathways others can follow. Storytelling helps bridge the gap between aspiration and action by providing concrete examples of how AI can be leveraged for social good, business growth, and community empowerment. Moreover, these narratives help challenge stereotypes and redefine what success looks like in the tech industry. By amplifying diverse voices, storytelling plays a critical role in creating an inclusive AI ecosystem that encourages everyone to contribute.

A Future Built on Inclusive Education

Inclusive AI education is not just about providing access; it is about creating systems that empower individuals to succeed. By addressing resource gaps, emphasizing ethical considerations, and fostering lifelong learning, we can build a future in which African American entrepreneurs are leaders in the AI economy. Empowering individuals through education transforms not only lives but also entire communities, driving innovation and economic growth.

The journey toward this inclusive future requires collective action from educators, policymakers, and industry leaders, but the rewards are well worth the effort. A diverse and inclusive AI ecosystem is one where everyone, regardless of their background, has the opportunity to gain experience, innovate, and succeed. By investing in education and ensuring that it is accessible and relevant, we can unlock the full potential of AI and build a future that benefits us all.

Empowering African American entrepreneurs through inclusive education creates ripples that extend beyond individual success. These leaders have the potential to create businesses that provide jobs, inspire future generations, and develop technologies that address pressing social challenges. An inclusive approach to AI education ensures that the innovations of tomorrow reflect the diverse needs and values of society, ultimately creating a more equitable and prosperous world for all.

Inspiration Bite: Angle Bush

Angle Bush is founder of Black Women in Artificial Intelligence (BWAI), an organization dedicated to empowering Black women in the AI sector through education, networking, and advocacy. BWAI provides resources and support to increase the representation and participation of Black women in AI, addressing systemic barriers and fostering a more inclusive tech community. Bush's work emphasizes the importance of diversity in AI development and the need for educational initiatives that equip underrepresented groups with the skills to thrive in the digital age.

Source: https://www.blackwomeninai.com/contact-8

Reflection Prompts

What gaps do you see in your current knowledge or skills? How can you begin to fill them?

How can education, whether formal or informal, empower you or your community to embrace AI and entrepreneurship?

What role can you play in mentoring or educating others to share the opportunities you've gained?

Chapter 9

Networking in the AI Era

> Surround yourself with only people who are going to lift you higher. – Oprah Winfrey, media executive and philanthropist.

For African American entrepreneurs navigating the complexities of the Artificial Intelligence (AI) landscape, building and leveraging strong networks is not merely advantageous, it is essential for success. This chapter explores the multifaceted nature of networking in the AI era, diving deeply into strategies, opportunities, and challenges unique to African American entrepreneurs as they forge connections, overcome barriers, and build bridges to lasting success.

ConnectWise AI: Networking in the AI Era

Networking in the modern age required more than just attending events, it needed intelligent matchmaking and strategic connection building. Recognizing this, Deja Howard founded ConnectWise AI, a platform that used AI to revolutionize professional networking for African American entrepreneurs. The platform employed machine learning algorithms to analyze users' backgrounds, business goals, and industry challenges, providing personalized recommendations for connections that could lead to meaningful partnerships. By identifying complementary skill sets and business opportunities, ConnectWise AI created a curated networking experience that amplified the potential for collaboration. Deja also incorporated natural language processing to facilitate introductions by generating personalized conversation starters, helping users break the ice during virtual networking events. By partnering with organizations like the National Black Chamber of Commerce and local community incubators, ConnectWise AI brought together professionals who could share resources, knowledge, and support. Deja's platform redefined networking as an intentional, AI-enhanced journey that was inclusive and effective, turning connections into collaborative opportunities for growth and impact.

AI Empowered, 91–98

Published under exclusive licence by Emerald Publishing Limited
doi:10.1108/978-1-83662-816-320251010

The Evolution of Networking in the Digital Age

Networking has always been the backbone of entrepreneurship, but the digital age has transformed how connections are created, maintained, and leveraged. Traditional face-to-face interactions have expanded into the virtual realm, enabling entrepreneurs to reach and nurture connections across the globe. This transformation has opened up unprecedented opportunities for African American entrepreneurs to access knowledge, resources, and collaborators that were once beyond their reach. It has redefined how they interact with the world, changing the very fabric of entrepreneurship itself.

Digital platforms like LinkedIn, Slack, and Clubhouse have become vital tools, breaking down geographical barriers and allowing African American entrepreneurs to participate in conversations from which they may have historically been excluded. The online space has redefined visibility, enabling them to connect with industry leaders, showcase their expertise, and be active participants in the AI ecosystem. It is through these digital platforms that African American entrepreneurs are empowered to create their own spaces, influence industry dialogue, and make significant strides in the AI world.

Social media, likewise, plays a critical role in the evolution of networking. By sharing their successes, innovations, and insights, African American entrepreneurs can craft influential personal brands that not only attract potential investors and partners but also inspire the next generation of innovators. In an environment where representation matters, showcasing accomplishments and narratives is crucial for inspiring others and opening doors that were previously closed. The digital age has thus redefined networking: it is no longer limited to local ecosystems; it is now an expansive, global force with the potential to connect those with aligned missions across continents and industries.

Building Networks That Empower Communities

While global networks are crucial, local and community-focused connections remain indispensable for African American entrepreneurs. Community-based networking initiatives create support ecosystems where resources are shared, mentorship is encouraged, and collaborative projects are fostered. Such networks provide a powerful sense of belonging, enabling entrepreneurs to address systemic challenges collectively and create environments where they can thrive on their own terms.

Organizations like AfroTech and Black in AI have played an instrumental role in fostering these community networks, crafting spaces where African Americans in technology can learn, grow, and thrive. These initiatives empower individuals, not just through professional development but also by instilling a sense of solidarity and collective advancement. They allow African American entrepreneurs to amplify their voices, advocate for inclusive policies, and challenge biases that persist in the AI industry. By creating networks that focus on the unique needs and challenges faced by Black entrepreneurs, these organizations lay the foundation for systemic change, enabling participants to rise together.

Local networking initiatives also help entrepreneurs by providing opportunities to engage with their immediate environment, tapping into local resources and ecosystems. These localized networks are critical for building on-the-ground support systems that understand the unique social, economic, and political landscapes in which African American entrepreneurs operate. By strengthening these local ties, entrepreneurs can harness the expertise, mentorship, and collaboration opportunities that their immediate communities have to offer.

Breaking Silos: Networking Across Industries

AI is not confined to any single discipline; it is an inherently multidisciplinary field with applications in healthcare, finance, education, transportation, and beyond. For African American entrepreneurs, establishing networks that extend across industries is critical for unlocking diverse opportunities and expanding into new markets. Cross-industry collaborations can be a game-changer, enabling entrepreneurs to develop products and solutions that are relevant across multiple sectors and are well-positioned to address real-world problems.

For example, an entrepreneur focused on healthcare AI could collaborate with doctors, hospitals, and data scientists to develop predictive diagnostic tools that could transform patient care. Similarly, an entrepreneur interested in education might partner with curriculum developers, school administrators, and teachers to create AI-driven learning platforms that provide personalized learning experiences for students. The value of these cross-industry collaborations lies in the diverse perspectives they bring, which fuel innovation and lead to groundbreaking solutions.

Cross-industry networking brings together people from different fields, each contributing unique knowledge and expertise to the table. Such interactions spark new ideas, allow entrepreneurs to see problems from new angles, and ultimately lead to the creation of better, more holistic solutions. African American entrepreneurs who adopt this approach can position themselves as pioneers capable of transforming multiple sectors and addressing the complexities of interconnected, systemic issues.

Mentorship Networks: Learning From Trailblazers

Mentorship is one of the most impactful forms of networking. African American entrepreneurs can gain invaluable insights from mentors who understand the unique challenges they face, offering both guidance and a gateway to their own established networks. Mentorship not only provides technical or business expertise but also serves as an emotional and psychological support system that can be critical for navigating systemic challenges and biases.

Mentorship takes many forms, from traditional one-on-one relationships to structured group mentorship programs. Platforms like Mentor Spaces connect African American professionals with experienced mentors in their fields, fostering opportunities for growth, guidance, and meaningful support. For entrepreneurs navigating the evolving AI space, mentors who have experience in both technology and business can help them overcome barriers, refine their strategies, and ultimately achieve their goals. These mentors become role models, showing by example that success is achievable and providing a framework for how to navigate the often-turbulent waters of entrepreneurship.

Mentorship can also have a ripple effect, where the knowledge and insights shared between mentor and mentee go on to impact broader communities. Mentees can take what they learn and mentor others, creating a chain reaction of knowledge dissemination and support. In the African American community, where access to mentors in the tech industry has historically been limited, this ripple effect can have a profound impact, inspiring new generations of entrepreneurs and contributing to a growing ecosystem of Black leaders in AI.

Conferences and Meetups: Building Connections in the AI Industry

Industry events like conferences, meetups, and hackathons are invaluable for networking in AI. Such gatherings bring together entrepreneurs, investors, technologists, and thought leaders, creating opportunities for learning, collaboration, and personal growth. These events are fertile grounds for idea generation, innovation, and exposure to cutting-edge advancements in technology.

For African American entrepreneurs, attending events like AfroTech, Black Enterprise TechConnext, or AI4ALL offers the opportunity to connect with like-minded individuals, share their work, and gain visibility within the tech community. Presenting at these events or participating in panels can further establish them as thought leaders, enhancing their professional networks and advancing their credibility in the AI space. Visibility is vital in an industry where representation is still lacking, and these platforms provide an opportunity for African American entrepreneurs to not only showcase their work but also inspire others who may see themselves represented for the first time.

Hackathons and meetups also provide hands-on opportunities to engage with emerging technology. By collaborating on projects in real time, entrepreneurs can develop and refine their skills, build relationships with other developers and technologists, and create products that may evolve into viable business ventures. These events help entrepreneurs to move beyond theory, providing real-world experiences that accelerate growth and learning.

Virtual Networks: Expanding Global Reach

The rise of virtual networking has fundamentally changed how entrepreneurs connect, particularly after the COVID-19 pandemic. For African American entrepreneurs, virtual platforms eliminate the financial and logistical barriers often associated with in-person events, enabling them to build global networks from their home offices. This virtual environment democratizes access to knowledge and collaboration opportunities, allowing for an unprecedented level of participation and inclusion.

Webinars, online forums, and virtual summits allow entrepreneurs to engage with international audiences, share their expertise, and explore markets beyond their local context. These virtual connections can lead to fruitful partnerships, funding opportunities, and access to global best practices. For example, an entrepreneur developing AI-driven agricultural tools might find collaborators in Africa or Asia, opening up a cross-continental dialogue that addresses shared challenges in innovative ways. Virtual networking can thus transform local ventures into global initiatives, multiplying their impact and reach.

The flexibility of virtual platforms also means that entrepreneurs can participate in multiple events, discussions, and forums that might have been impossible to attend in person due to time, cost, or distance. African American entrepreneurs can engage with these platforms to continuously engage with global audiences, expanding their horizons and staying informed about the latest trends, challenges, and opportunities in AI. This global perspective is invaluable in an industry that evolves as rapidly as AI, where staying ahead of the curve is key to success.

The Power of Peer-to-Peer Networking

Peer-to-peer networking often goes unnoticed but can be incredibly impactful for African American entrepreneurs. Building relationships with fellow entrepreneurs fosters collaboration, knowledge sharing, and mutual support, creating a safety net that can be crucial when facing systemic biases or navigating an underrepresented market. These peer connections are grounded in shared experiences and mutual understanding, which can be empowering in an environment that is not always welcoming.

These peer networks provide a platform for candid discussions about unique challenges, such as securing funding, navigating implicit biases, or finding the right partners in an underrepresented market. Such connections empower entrepreneurs, enabling them to work together to overcome barriers and achieve collective growth. Peer-to-peer support systems are crucial for providing encouragement, sharing resources, and creating opportunities for collaboration that benefit all participants. They create an environment where entrepreneurs can learn from each other's mistakes, celebrate each other's successes, and move forward together.

Peer networking can also be a powerful mechanism for holding each other accountable. In a challenging industry like AI, where progress often requires resilience and perseverance, having a group of peers who can provide honest feedback, encourage accountability, and share insights can be the difference between moving forward and stagnating. African American entrepreneurs can draw strength from these networks, ensuring that they are supported not only professionally but also personally.

Investing in Long-Term Relationships

Networking is not just about initial introductions – it is about cultivating lasting relationships that evolve and grow over time. For African American entrepreneurs, success in networking comes from remaining engaged with their communities, continually contributing value, and intentionally building trust. Long-term relationships are built on a foundation of mutual respect, consistent engagement, and a genuine interest in each other's success.

Long-term relationships with mentors, peers, collaborators, and even competitors can yield unexpected opportunities, from joint ventures to career-defining mentorship roles. By prioritizing these relationships and recognizing that meaningful connections often take time to develop, African American entrepreneurs can build a network that consistently supports and amplifies their efforts. It is often through these deeper, sustained connections that the most impactful opportunities arise – whether it be a lucrative partnership, a new market opportunity, or simply someone willing to vouch for you in a critical moment.

In an industry like AI, which is both highly competitive and constantly evolving, long-term relationships can provide a stability that helps entrepreneurs weather the ups and downs. These relationships can also be the source of ongoing inspiration, offering new perspectives and insights that keep entrepreneurs motivated and focused on their long-term vision. African American entrepreneurs, in particular, benefit from these strong ties, as they provide a support system that is sensitive to the unique challenges they face, fostering resilience and perseverance.

Networking as Advocacy: Amplifying Voices for Change

Networking is not merely a tool for personal advancement, it is also a platform for advocacy. African American entrepreneurs can use their networks to amplify their voices, challenge systemic inequities, and push for lasting change within the AI industry. Networks provide a collective strength that can be used to influence policies, practices, and perceptions, creating a more inclusive and equitable landscape.

By advocating for inclusive hiring practices, participating in conversations around ethical AI, or mentoring future innovators, African American entrepreneurs can use their connections to influence the tech ecosystem toward one that values diversity, equity, and inclusion. Through their advocacy, they can lay the groundwork for a future where opportunities in AI are accessible to all, and where Black innovators are recognized for their contributions and provided with the opportunities they deserve. Advocacy within networks turns individual successes into collective victories, reshaping the industry for future generations.

Networking also enables African American entrepreneurs to participate in important discussions about the societal implications of AI, such as bias in algorithms, data privacy, and the ethical use of technology. By leveraging their networks to join these conversations, they can contribute valuable perspectives that may otherwise be overlooked, ensuring that AI is developed and deployed in ways that are fair and beneficial for all communities.

A Vision for Inclusive Networking

The future of networking lies in inclusivity, collaboration, and empowerment. For African American entrepreneurs, it is about building networks that reflect their values and aspirations while actively challenging the systemic barriers that have historically excluded them. Inclusive networking means intentionally creating spaces where everyone has a seat at the table and ensuring that voices that have been marginalized are heard, respected, and valued.

By embracing digital platforms, fostering community-based networks, and cultivating long-term relationships, African American entrepreneurs can harness the power of networking to drive innovation, growth, and social impact. These networks are more than just connections – they are catalysts for change, capable of creating lasting value for themselves and future generations. Inclusive networks are the foundation upon which a diverse and equitable AI industry can be built, one where opportunity is not limited by background or identity, but where talent, passion, and dedication are the only prerequisites for success.

The Power of Connections: A Catalyst for Growth

In the AI industry, networking serves as a powerful catalyst for growth, providing entrepreneurs with access to vital knowledge, collaboration opportunities, funding, mentorship, and potential customers. For African American entrepreneurs, who often face additional barriers in the tech industry, strong networks can be instrumental in overcoming challenges and amplifying their impact in the AI space.

Networking requires a strategic and persistent approach. Authenticity, consistency, value addition, follow-up, and diversity are essential for building meaningful relationships. By actively engaging in networks, whether global or community-based, African American entrepreneurs can foster supportive ecosystems that propel their ventures forward. A well-crafted network is not just a collection of contacts but a living, breathing ecosystem that offers opportunities for growth, learning, and support at every stage of an entrepreneur's journey.

Successful networking also requires that entrepreneurs give as much as they take. Adding value to others in their network, whether through sharing knowledge, offering assistance, or simply being a supportive voice, ensures that relationships are mutually beneficial and long-lasting. For African American entrepreneurs, the strength of their networks is not only in the number of connections but in the quality and depth of these relationships, which can lead to transformative opportunities that benefit both individuals and the broader community.

Building a Network of Empowerment

In the era of AI, networks are more than just professional connections; they are lifelines that provide access to opportunities, resources, and knowledge that can make the difference between success and stagnation. For African American entrepreneurs, the goal is not only to navigate the complexities of the AI landscape but also to shape a future where their contributions are recognized and valued. Networks are the bridges that help close gaps, overcome barriers, and pave the way for meaningful participation in the AI revolution.

By welcoming collaboration, community engagement, and advocacy, African American entrepreneurs can build bridges to success, not only for themselves but for the generations of innovators that will follow. These connections have the power to transform individual lives and, collectively, help redefine an industry that has long been characterized by barriers instead of bridges. The future of AI will be determined by those who are willing to reach out, connect, and uplift others, creating a vibrant, inclusive ecosystem that drives innovation and equity.

To ensure the continued growth and empowerment of African American entrepreneurs in AI, it is crucial that these networks are nurtured and expanded. Entrepreneurs must be proactive in seeking out opportunities, engaging in industry conversations, and advocating for inclusiveness at every turn. The potential for impact is vast, and the networks built today will shape the opportunities of tomorrow. By working together, African American entrepreneurs can ensure that the AI industry not only benefits from their perspectives but is fundamentally transformed by their presence, leadership, and vision.

Inspiration Bite: Renée Cummings

Renée Cummings is an AI ethicist and criminologist who serves as a Professor of Practice at the University of Virginia's School of Data Science. She is also a nonresident senior fellow at The Brookings Institution and a distinguished member of the World Economic Forum's Data Equity Council. Cummings' work focuses on promoting ethical AI development and ensuring diverse representation in AI systems. She emphasizes the importance of inclusive innovation and the ethical implications of data on society, advocating for justice-oriented and trauma-informed AI.

Source: https://www.brookings.edu/people/renee-cummings

Reflection Prompts

Who in your current network can help you achieve your goals, and how can you strengthen those relationships?

What steps can you take to build connections with people in the AI and tech industries?

How can you create or join a supportive community of like-minded entrepreneurs to share resources and insights?

Chapter 10

Global Perspectives on African American Entrepreneurship in AI

> AI was more of an opportunity than a challenge for the Global South, but digital literacy and the cost of devices need to be addressed. – Paula Ingabire, Rwanda's Minister of Information Communication Technology and Innovation.

The African diaspora, spanning continents and cultures, represents a dynamic force in the global economy, with entrepreneurship forming a core pillar of its contributions. Within the realm of Artificial Intelligence (AI), members of the African diaspora have begun to put to use their unique perspectives, cultural heritage, and adaptability to establish themselves as innovators in the technology sector. However, this journey is fraught with distinct trends and challenges that define their experience.

Empowerment ArtIn: Global Perspectives on Black Entrepreneurship

Empowerment ArtIn sought to connect African American entrepreneurs with their counterparts across the African diaspora, creating a global support network driven by shared experiences. Using machine learning to analyze and connect people based on complementary skills and business needs, the platform fostered international collaborations and cross-border mentorships. An AI-based recommendation engine matched startup founders in the United States with established African entrepreneurs who had overcome similar challenges. By leveraging the power of storytelling and virtual reality, Empowerment ArtIn allowed users to immerse themselves in each other's entrepreneurial journeys, providing a firsthand understanding of different markets, challenges, and cultural nuances. Through this global network, entrepreneurs not only exchanged business insights but also created supply chains that crossed continents, opening new market opportunities and fostering a sense of unity across the diaspora. Empowerment ArtIn turned what was once a fragmented landscape into a thriving, interconnected web of Black entrepreneurship.

AI Empowered, 99–103

doi:10.1108/978-1-83662-816-320251011

Background

One significant trend among Black entrepreneurs in AI is the emphasis on inclusive technology development. Many within the diaspora focus on creating AI systems that address the specific needs of underrepresented communities, from improving healthcare accessibility to refining educational tools. This commitment to inclusivity stems from a profound understanding of systemic inequities and a desire to rectify these through innovative technological solutions. Such innovations are not only about bridging gaps but also about creating new pathways for growth and development, contributing to a more equitable global technology landscape.

Yet, systemic barriers persist. Funding disparities remain a notable obstacle; Black entrepreneurs often face difficulties in securing venture capital compared to their white counterparts. Structural biases in funding networks, compounded by a lack of representation in investment decision-making roles, exacerbate this issue. Additionally, many Black-led startups encounter challenges in accessing advanced AI resources, such as high-performance computing capabilities, data repositories, and skilled talent pools. These hurdles often necessitate a level of ingenuity and adaptability that fosters innovative problem-solving, pushing entrepreneurs to explore unconventional solutions and partnerships.

Despite these challenges, the diaspora demonstrates resilience through creative adaptation. Grassroots networking, collaboration within global Black tech communities, and participation in accelerators tailored to minority-led businesses have helped many navigate these barriers. Furthermore, a growing focus on partnerships with African governments and multinational organizations reflects a strategic pivot toward leveraging the continent's rising technological infrastructure. This proactive engagement demonstrates a deeper understanding of how AI can be tailored to address not only local challenges but also global market demands, further embedding Black entrepreneurs in the wider AI ecosystem.

Moreover, the diaspora's ability to build bridges between regions is becoming increasingly apparent. African entrepreneurs in AI are fostering connections with their counterparts in Europe, North America, and Asia, sharing resources and insights that drive innovation across borders. These transcontinental collaborations are helping to mitigate some of the systemic barriers, offering access to funding, mentorship, and advanced research facilities. This ability to navigate multiple cultural and economic landscapes highlights the potential of Black entrepreneurs to act as global connectors, aligning diverse markets and opportunities.

Success Stories From Africa and the Caribbean

Africa and the Caribbean have emerged as hotspots for innovation, producing success stories that exemplify the potential of Black entrepreneurship in AI. These regions, marked by diverse socioeconomic conditions, demonstrate how challenges can be transformed into opportunities through ingenuity and determination.

In Africa, entrepreneurs have harnessed AI to tackle pressing issues, including agriculture, healthcare, and urban development. For example, companies like

Zipline in Rwanda have revolutionized medical supply delivery through AI-driven drone technology, saving countless lives in remote areas. Similarly, Nigeria's data analytics company Data Science Nigeria has empowered young people by providing AI education and fostering an ecosystem of innovation. These initiatives not only showcase entrepreneurial success but also highlight the role of AI in fostering development.

In Kenya, startups like Twiga Foods are using AI to optimize supply chain management, ensuring food security by connecting farmers directly with markets. This innovative use of technology has reduced waste and improved efficiency, illustrating the profound impact of AI when applied to local challenges. Similarly, South Africa's Aerobotics is leveraging AI and machine learning to assist farmers in monitoring crop health and maximizing yields, demonstrating the scalability of such technologies in addressing global agricultural needs.

A tech firm in Ghana deployed to improve educational outcomes by using AI-driven voice assistants to deliver content in local languages. These efforts are vital in a region where language diversity often poses barriers to education. Entrepreneurs are demonstrating how culturally attuned technologies can bridge these divides, ensuring that the benefits of AI reach even the most marginalized populations.

The Caribbean has also contributed significantly to this narrative. Entrepreneurs in Jamaica, Barbados, and Trinidad and Tobago have used AI to advance tourism, agriculture, and disaster management. Startups such as ListenMi, a Jamaican company specializing in AI-driven audio solutions, have tapped into global markets while maintaining a strong cultural identity. Meanwhile, disaster-prone regions have seen the emergence of AI tools that predict and mitigate the impact of hurricanes, offering life-saving interventions rooted in data-driven decision-making. In addition, small island nations are leveraging AI to optimize resource management, tackling challenges such as energy consumption and water distribution with a focus on sustainability.

These success stories are not isolated incidents but part of a broader pattern of innovation fueled by necessity and resourcefulness. By capitalizing on local knowledge, cultural insights, and international networks, Black entrepreneurs in Africa and the Caribbean are setting a precedent for future generations of innovators. Their ability to address pressing local issues while simultaneously achieving global recognition reflects a powerful duality that defines the spirit of entrepreneurship within these regions. Furthermore, these successes inspire collaborations that transcend geographical boundaries, fostering a global movement of Black-led innovation.

Lessons From the Global South

The Global South offers a unique lens through which to examine the intersection of AI and entrepreneurship. Regions within the Global South, often characterized by limited resources but abundant creativity, reveal the complexities of adopting and implementing AI technologies in less developed contexts. For Black entrepreneurs, these lessons are invaluable, both as a source of inspiration and as a framework for collaboration.

One key lesson is the importance of frugality and efficiency. Entrepreneurs in the Global South have developed solutions that maximize impact with minimal resources. For example, in India and parts of Southeast Asia, AI-driven microfinance platforms have transformed access to credit for underserved populations. Similarly, in Latin America, AI-powered agricultural tools are helping smallholder farmers optimize yields while conserving resources. These innovations demonstrate the potential for high-impact solutions that address systemic challenges without relying on extravagant budgets or infrastructure.

Another critical insight is the value of community-driven development. In many Global South contexts, technology adoption is driven not by top-down mandates but by grassroots movements. Black entrepreneurs can take cues from this approach, fostering strong community involvement in the design and deployment of AI solutions. By ensuring that technologies are culturally sensitive and locally relevant, entrepreneurs can drive deeper and more sustainable adoption. This focus on grassroots engagement is particularly relevant in diverse communities where trust and inclusivity can dictate the success of new technologies.

Finally, the Global South highlights the significance of policy advocacy and capacity building. For AI to thrive, robust policy frameworks and a skilled workforce are essential. Entrepreneurs in the African diaspora can contribute to and benefit from global efforts to build AI literacy, advocate for fair regulations, and establish ethical guidelines. Collaborative initiatives with governments, NGOs, and academic institutions can help bridge the gap between technology potential and practical implementation. By aligning efforts with the broader Global South agenda, Black entrepreneurs can position themselves as key players in shaping the ethical and operational landscape of AI adoption worldwide.

In addition, there is an opportunity for reciprocal learning. Black entrepreneurs can not only adopt lessons from the Global South but also share their unique approaches to overcoming systemic barriers, creating a two-way exchange that enriches both ecosystems. Such collaboration ensures that technological advancements are both equitable and impactful, reinforcing a shared commitment to leveraging AI for the greater good. This mutual exchange builds a network of global solidarity, where diverse voices contribute to a common goal of inclusive and sustainable technological progress.

Toward a Unified Future

The global landscape of Black entrepreneurship in AI is one of challenges and triumphs, resilience and innovation. From the African diaspora's creative adaptations to the success stories emerging from Africa and the Caribbean to the lessons gleaned from the Global South, a clear picture emerges: Black entrepreneurs are poised to shape the future of AI, not as passive participants but as active architects.

By fostering networks of collaboration, championing inclusivity, and drawing on the rich lessons of global contexts, Black entrepreneurs can ensure their voices resonate in the AI revolution. The road ahead is not without obstacles, but it is also paved with boundless opportunities to transform lives, redefine industries, and inspire generations to come.

The future of Black entrepreneurship in AI lies not just in overcoming challenges but in redefining the narrative of technological innovation. By building solutions that are inclusive, sustainable, and impactful, Black entrepreneurs have the potential to lead a global movement that bridges divides and uplifts communities. In doing so, they will continue to prove that diversity and innovation are not just compatible but essential to the future of AI and the world at large.

As the world moves deeper into the age of AI, the contributions of Black entrepreneurs will be instrumental in shaping a more equitable and forward-thinking technological landscape. By embracing their heritage, leveraging global networks, and remaining steadfast in their commitment to inclusive innovation, Black entrepreneurs in AI are not only solving today's problems but also laying the foundation for a brighter and more inclusive future for all.

Inspiration Bite: will.i.am

Beyond his successful music career, will.i.am has ventured into technology entrepreneurship, particularly in the AI space. He founded i.am+, a company that develops AI-powered products, including the AI voice assistant Omega. will.i.am advocates for diversity in technology and emphasizes the importance of representation in AI development. His work reflects a global perspective on Black entrepreneurship in AI, highlighting the intersection of creativity and technology.

Source: https://www.semafor.com/article/10/04/2024/talking-through-ai-and-the-future-of-music-with-william

Reflection Prompts

How do you see yourself or your business contributing to the global conversation on AI and entrepreneurship?

What lessons can you learn from entrepreneurs in other countries who have faced similar challenges?

How can you build partnerships or collaborations that extend beyond your local community or region?

Chapter 11

Ethical AI and Responsible Innovation

> I've learned that people will forget what you said, people will forget what you did, but people will never forget how you made them feel. – Maya Angelou, poet and civil rights activist.

Artificial Intelligence (AI) has emerged as a transformative force across industries, promising to enhance productivity, automate complex processes, and unlock new possibilities in areas ranging from healthcare to finance. However, with this promise comes significant ethical challenges that demand urgent attention. Among the most pressing issues are biases embedded in algorithms, often reflecting and amplifying societal inequalities. These biases manifest in ways that disproportionately affect marginalized communities, leading to discriminatory outcomes in hiring practices, credit approvals, predictive policing, and more.

The roots of bias in AI lie in the data these systems are trained on and the perspectives of those developing the technologies. Training data often mirrors historical inequalities, while the underrepresentation of diverse voices in AI development perpetuates a narrow worldview. For instance, facial recognition systems have demonstrated higher error rates when identifying individuals with darker skin tones, a direct result of underrepresentation in training datasets. These inequities underscore the necessity of grounding AI innovation in ethics, ensuring that technological progress benefits all members of society equitably. Beyond fairness, the ethical dimensions of AI also involve considerations of privacy, autonomy, and transparency. These facets form a complex web of challenges requiring collective action from developers, policymakers, and communities to build trust in AI systems.

The importance of ethics in AI is paramount, especially as these systems become integral to decision-making processes that shape lives. Ethical lapses in AI can have far-reaching consequences, eroding public trust and exacerbating social divisions. Addressing these challenges requires a proactive approach that incorporates ethical considerations from the outset, ensuring that innovation is guided by principles that uphold human dignity and equity. The discussion surrounding AI ethics is not just an abstract debate but a critical conversation that defines the trajectory of technological progress in the 21st century.

AI Empowered, 105–111

Published under exclusive licence by Emerald Publishing Limited
doi:10.1108/978-1-83662-816-320251012

Unified Network AI: Building Ethical AI and Responsible Innovation

In an era where AI ethics often seemed like an afterthought, Unified Network AI embeds ethical considerations into every stage of AI development. Unified Network AI was a collaborative platform where AI developers, community representatives, and ethicists worked together to build technology that aligned with community values. By employing AI to simulate and analyze the societal impacts of proposed innovations, Unified Network AI provided insights into how technologies would affect marginalized groups before they were even deployed. It also used blockchain to maintain transparency and accountability, ensuring that all development steps were visible to stakeholders. By focusing on responsible innovation, Unified Network AI empowered African American entrepreneurs to lead by example, creating AI systems that prioritized fairness, equity, and social good. Unified Network AI's work highlighted the importance of involving diverse voices in technological development, demonstrating that ethical AI wasn't just possible; it was necessary for creating lasting, positive change.

Bias in AI and African American Entrepreneurs

African American entrepreneurs occupy a unique and powerful position in addressing AI bias. Their lived experiences provide invaluable insights into systemic inequities and the limitations of technology designed without inclusivity in mind. These entrepreneurs can identify the subtleties of algorithmic discrimination and envision solutions that prioritize fairness and equity.

For example, African American founders in the tech space often approach innovation with a dual lens: one of technical capability and another rooted in cultural awareness. This perspective enables them to spot issues others might overlook, such as the exclusion of minority groups from mainstream datasets or the perpetuation of stereotypes through algorithmic recommendations. By actively engaging with these challenges, African American entrepreneurs can lead the charge in designing AI systems that are not only functional but also ethical and inclusive.

The contributions of African American entrepreneurs extend beyond technical fixes; they bring an advocacy-driven approach to AI development. They emphasize the importance of ethical decision-making processes and collaborate with researchers, civil rights organizations, and other stakeholders to shape AI governance. By serving as both creators and watchdogs, they push for systemic change, demonstrating that diversity in leadership is critical to solving complex societal issues.

Moreover, these entrepreneurs can serve as advocates for greater diversity in AI development teams and decision-making bodies, fostering environments where a variety of perspectives shape technological solutions. Their leadership challenges the status quo, paving the way for a new generation of AI systems that are reflective of the diversity inherent in society. The intersection of their enterprising spirit and cultural insights positions them to lead transformative changes in the AI landscape, inspiring others to prioritize ethical considerations in their endeavors.

African American entrepreneurs also play a crucial role in raising awareness about the broader societal implications of biased AI. By using platforms to share their stories and insights, they highlight the real-world impact of algorithmic inequities and mobilize support for systemic change. Their efforts underscore the interconnectedness of technological innovation and social justice, emphasizing that progress in one area must not come at the expense of equity in another.

Strategies for Ethical AI Development

To build AI systems that prioritize fairness and inclusivity, entrepreneurs must adopt robust frameworks and practices. Ethical AI development begins with intentionality: designing systems with a clear understanding of potential biases and their impact. Below are key strategies for ensuring responsible innovation.

Inclusive Data Practices

Data is the backbone of AI, and ensuring its diversity is critical to mitigating bias. Entrepreneurs should actively seek out and incorporate datasets that represent varied demographics, geographies, and cultural contexts. This process involves identifying gaps in existing data, partnering with organizations that can provide underrepresented perspectives, and continually refining datasets to ensure balance. Effective data management practices should also prioritize data quality and ethical sourcing, ensuring that the information collected respects privacy and consent.

Inclusive data practices also require vigilance against unintentional bias introduced during data processing and model training. Entrepreneurs should employ techniques such as data augmentation, bias correction algorithms, and rigorous testing to identify and mitigate disparities. By taking a holistic approach to data management, developers can ensure that AI systems are not only accurate but also equitable in their decision-making processes.

Transparency and Accountability

Ethical AI requires transparency at every stage of development. Entrepreneurs should document their processes, articulate the limitations of their models, and provide stakeholders with clear explanations of how decisions are made. Accountability mechanisms, such as third-party audits and public reporting, ensure that developers remain vigilant against ethical lapses. Transparency is also crucial for fostering trust among end-users, as it allows them to understand and question the decisions made by AI systems.

Establishing accountability involves creating robust feedback loops where end-users and stakeholders can report concerns or flag potential biases. Entrepreneurs should treat these feedback mechanisms as integral to the innovation process, using them to refine their models and enhance their ethical integrity. By embedding accountability into the core of AI development, businesses can create systems that are both trustworthy and adaptable.

Human-in-the-Loop Systems

Introducing human oversight into AI systems can help prevent unintended consequences. By involving diverse teams in the review and validation of AI outputs, entrepreneurs can catch biases that automated processes might miss. Human-in-the-loop approaches also allow for continuous feedback and adjustment, ensuring that systems evolve responsibly. This iterative approach integrates ethical review as a core component of the development lifecycle, balancing efficiency with fairness.

Human-in-the-loop systems are particularly valuable in high-stakes applications such as healthcare, criminal justice, and hiring. In these contexts, the stakes of error are too high to rely solely on automated decision-making. By integrating human judgment into these systems, entrepreneurs can ensure that ethical considerations remain at the forefront of their operations, minimizing the risk of harm while maximizing societal benefit.

Ethical Frameworks and Governance

Adopting established ethical frameworks, such as the principles outlined by the AI Ethics Guidelines of organizations like the European Commission or the IEEE, provides a solid foundation for responsible innovation. Entrepreneurs should also establish internal governance structures, such as ethics boards, to evaluate the societal implications of their technologies. Proactive governance helps anticipate potential risks and ensures that ethical considerations are not an afterthought but an integral part of innovation.

Ethics boards and advisory committees should include representatives from diverse backgrounds and disciplines, ensuring that a variety of perspectives are brought to bear on complex issues. By fostering cross-disciplinary collaboration, entrepreneurs can anticipate and address ethical challenges more effectively, creating AI systems that are not only innovative but also socially responsible.

Community Engagement

Involving the communities affected by AI solutions is essential for building trust and ensuring relevance. Entrepreneurs should prioritize collaboration with stakeholders, including marginalized groups, to co-create solutions that address their needs and concerns. This participatory approach ensures that AI serves as a tool for empowerment rather than oppression. Community-driven feedback mechanisms can also uncover hidden biases, offering insights that developers might not access otherwise.

Community engagement also fosters a sense of ownership among stakeholders, encouraging them to actively participate in the ongoing refinement of AI systems. By treating community members as partners rather than passive recipients of technology, entrepreneurs can build stronger relationships and create solutions that are truly inclusive. This approach not only enhances the ethical integrity of AI systems but also strengthens their social impact.

Case Studies

Case Study 1: Algorithmic Fairness in Lending

A fintech startup founded by an African American entrepreneur tackled the issue of bias in credit scoring algorithms. Recognizing that traditional credit systems often disadvantage minorities, the startup developed an alternative scoring model that incorporates nontraditional metrics such as rent payment histories and utility bills. This approach expanded access to credit for underserved communities while maintaining rigorous standards of financial responsibility. The startup's methodology involved continuous testing and refinement of the model to ensure equity, setting a new benchmark for fairness in financial technology.

The startup also invested in community outreach programs to educate potential users about their rights and the benefits of alternative credit models. By combining technological innovation with grassroots advocacy, the company not only improved access to credit but also empowered individuals to make informed financial decisions. This holistic approach underscores the transformative potential of ethical AI in addressing systemic inequities.

Case Study 2: Inclusive Health Diagnostics

Another initiative led by a diverse team of founders focused on reducing racial disparities in healthcare diagnostics. By curating a training dataset that included images and data from underrepresented groups, the team improved the accuracy of their AI model for detecting skin conditions across different skin tones. This innovation not only enhanced diagnostic precision but also addressed long-standing inequities in dermatology. Their approach extended to developing educational resources for clinicians, empowering them to utilize AI insights effectively and inclusively.

The team also collaborated with medical schools and professional associations to promote awareness about the importance of diversity in healthcare AI. By embedding their work within broader efforts to advance health equity, the initiative amplified its impact, demonstrating how technology can serve as a catalyst for systemic change in critical sectors like healthcare.

Case Study 3: Ethical AI in Recruitment

An African American entrepreneur launched a hiring platform designed to eliminate bias in recruitment processes. The platform used anonymized profiles to focus on candidates' skills and experiences rather than demographic indicators. Additionally, the system was regularly audited to identify and correct any emerging biases, setting a standard for ethical practices in the recruitment technology space. The platform's success highlighted the value of integrating ethical principles with technological innovation to transform hiring landscapes.

The entrepreneur also partnered with organizations advocating for workplace diversity to ensure the platform remained aligned with best practices and evolving societal expectations. This collaborative approach not only enhanced the credibility of the platform but also reinforced its commitment to creating equitable opportunities for all job seekers.

Case Study 4: AI for Educational Equity

A tech startup founded by a team of educators and engineers addressed the disparity in access to quality educational tools. They developed an AI-driven learning platform tailored to the needs of underrepresented students. The system incorporated adaptive learning techniques and culturally relevant content, ensuring that the platform resonated with diverse learners. By leveraging community partnerships and teacher input, the startup maintained a consistent focus on equity and empowerment, making education accessible to a broader audience.

The platform's developers also invested in longitudinal studies to track its impact on student outcomes over time. These studies provided valuable insights into the effectiveness of the platform, enabling continuous improvement and reinforcing its commitment to delivering meaningful results. By prioritizing evidence-based practices, the startup set a high standard for ethical innovation in the education sector.

The journey toward ethical AI and responsible innovation is both challenging and essential. As the influence of AI grows, so does the responsibility to ensure that it reflects the values of fairness, inclusivity, and justice. African American entrepreneurs, with their unique perspectives and experiences, are at the forefront of this movement, driving meaningful change in the tech landscape. By adopting ethical frameworks, championing diversity, and engaging with communities, they can create AI solutions that empower rather than marginalize, setting a precedent for a more equitable technological future.

The path forward demands collaboration and persistence. Policymakers, technologists, and community leaders must unite to address the ethical challenges posed by AI. By fostering a culture of accountability and inclusivity, society can harness AI's potential while safeguarding against its risks. The work of African American entrepreneurs and other advocates serves as an inspiring blueprint for building a technological future that prioritizes humanity, equity, and justice above all else.

The journey ahead is not without obstacles, but it is one that holds immense promise. By centering ethics at the heart of AI development, society can transform challenges into opportunities, ensuring that technological progress serves as a force for good in a rapidly changing world.

Inspiration Bite: Angela Heath

Angela Heath, CEO, TKC Incorporated, a company that develops AI no-code tools aimed at assisting Black and Brown solopreneurs. Her work focuses on promoting responsible innovation in AI by providing accessible tools that empower underrepresented entrepreneurs. Heath's initiatives emphasize the importance of ethical AI development and the need for inclusive technological solutions that address the unique challenges faced by minority entrepreneurs.

Source: https://tkcincorporated.com/meet-angela/

Reflection Prompts

How do you define ethical business practices, and how can you ensure your work aligns with those values?

What risks or biases might your use of AI introduce, and how can you mitigate them?

How can you contribute to creating technology that not only succeeds but also uplifts African American and other marginalized communities?

Chapter 12

Leveraging AI for Frugal Innovation

> By integrating AI into frugal innovation strategies, organizations can achieve sustainable growth by doing better with less. – Navi Radjou

The concept of frugal innovation, creating cost-effective, high-quality solutions by maximizing limited resources, has emerged as a powerful strategy for those looking to make a significant impact without substantial capital. When combined with the transformative capabilities of Artificial Intelligence (AI), frugal innovation becomes an even more potent tool, enabling entrepreneurs to overcome traditional barriers and tailor their offerings to the unique needs of their communities.

This chapter explores how African American entrepreneurs can harness AI to drive frugal innovation, ultimately fostering business growth and contributing to community development. By embracing this approach, entrepreneurs can not only reduce costs but also deliver products and services that resonate deeply with their target markets.

AI Frugal Innovators: Leveraging Technology for Resource-Limited Environments

Kwame Adebanjo believed in the power of ingenuity under constraint. He founded AI Frugal Innovators, an incubator that nurtured resourceful entrepreneurs who could make use of AI to solve pressing issues with limited resources. The program focused on equipping innovators in economically marginalized areas with AI-driven tools to develop solutions that addressed their communities' specific needs. From AI-powered water purification systems in underserved neighborhoods to predictive crop management solutions that maximized agricultural output without expensive machinery, Kwame's incubator turned challenges into opportunities. By utilizing cost-effective AI tools like open-source machine learning platforms, AI Frugal Innovators transformed resource limitations into a catalyst for creativity, empowering individuals to solve problems with local relevance and global applicability. This approach didn't just encourage

AI Empowered, 113–117

Published under exclusive licence by Emerald Publishing Limited
doi:10.1108/978-1-83662-816-320251013

entrepreneurship; it made technology meaningful by anchoring it in the everyday lives of people who most needed its benefits.

Understanding Frugal Innovation

Frugal innovation is more than just cost-cutting; it's a mindset that prioritizes simplicity, resourcefulness, and sustainability. It involves reimagining products and services to make them more accessible and affordable without compromising on quality. This approach encourages entrepreneurs to rethink traditional business models, creatively gather available resources, and focus on essential features that provide maximum value to customers.

For African American entrepreneurs, frugal innovation presents a valuable avenue to address systemic challenges such as limited access to capital and resources. By concentrating on core needs and employing innovative problem-solving techniques, they can develop impactful solutions that not only meet market demands but also contribute to societal advancement.

The Role of AI in Frugal Innovation

AI has revolutionized various industries by offering tools that enhance efficiency, reduce costs, and enable the creation of intelligent products and services. In the context of frugal innovation, AI serves as a catalyst that amplifies the ability to do more with less.

One significant way AI contributes to frugal innovation is through cost reduction. By automating repetitive tasks, AI-powered software streamlines operations like administrative duties, customer service interactions, and supply chain management. This automation reduces operational expenses and frees up resources that can be redirected toward growth and development initiatives.

AI also enhances product development by facilitating rapid prototyping and personalization. Entrepreneurs can use AI tools to simulate product designs and functionalities, thereby reducing the time and costs associated with physical prototyping. Additionally, AI algorithms can analyze customer data to tailor products and services to individual preferences, increasing customer satisfaction without incurring substantial additional expenses.

Expanding market reach is another area where AI proves invaluable. Through digital marketing automation, AI optimizes advertising campaigns by effectively targeting potential customers, maximizing the return on investment. Language processing technologies enable businesses to communicate with diverse markets, breaking language barriers without the need for multilingual staff. Furthermore, AI chatbots provide around-the-clock customer support, enhancing the customer experience while keeping overhead costs low.

Opportunities and Challenges

The integration of AI in frugal innovation opens up numerous opportunities for African American entrepreneurs to make a significant impact in their communities and beyond. By leveraging AI to develop frugal solutions, entrepreneurs can create products and services that directly address the unique challenges faced by their communities.

One prominent example is AI-driven financial services. Access to financial products remains a challenge in many underserved areas, but AI can enable more inclusive financial solutions. Startups can deploy AI-based credit scoring algorithms to assess creditworthiness for people with limited financial histories, providing them with access to loans. These solutions can empower individuals to build businesses, invest in education, or improve their standard of living, effectively using AI to reduce economic inequality.

Similarly, AI-powered educational tools can bridge the educational divide. Entrepreneurs can make use of AI to create adaptive learning platforms that adjust to the pace and learning style of individual students. This allows those in under-resourced communities to access personalized education at low cost, helping to close the knowledge gap and promote educational equity.

Frugal innovation empowers entrepreneurs to maximize limited resources, making it possible to launch and grow businesses without substantial capital. By utilizing AI tools to automate processes and reduce operational costs, entrepreneurs can adopt lean startup models that minimize initial investment requirements. Additionally, AI can enhance crowdfunding efforts by identifying and targeting the most receptive audience segments, increasing the effectiveness of fundraising campaigns.

However, the adoption of AI in frugal innovation also brings challenges. One significant challenge is equitable access to AI technologies. High upfront costs of hardware, the need for reliable internet, and limited access to AI talent can hinder progress. Addressing these issues will require partnerships with academic institutions, nonprofits, and government bodies to foster better infrastructure, provide affordable technology, and establish educational programs that upskill entrepreneurs for the AI-driven market.

Strategies for Leveraging AI in Frugal Innovation

Utilizing open-source AI tools can significantly reduce expenses related to software licensing. Platforms like TensorFlow and PyTorch provide robust resources for developing machine learning models, enabling entrepreneurs to build sophisticated AI applications without incurring high costs. These tools offer flexibility and scalability, making them suitable for businesses at various stages of development.

Gaining a foundational understanding of AI technologies empowers entrepreneurs to implement solutions independently and make informed decisions. Online courses offered by platforms like Coursera and Udemy provide affordable access to quality education on AI topics. Participating in workshops and webinars can also offer practical insights and keep entrepreneurs updated on the latest advancements in the field.

Forming partnerships with AI professionals and organizations can bridge knowledge gaps and provide valuable support. Collaborating with universities and research institutions grants access to expertise and resources that might otherwise be unavailable. Engaging with tech hubs and incubators can also facilitate networking opportunities and provide mentorship, accelerating the growth and development of entrepreneurial ventures.

Utilizing AI-as-a-Service platforms allows entrepreneurs to access advanced AI capabilities on a pay-as-you-go basis. Cloud-based services from providers like Amazon Web Services (AWS), Google Cloud, and Microsoft Azure offer scalable solutions without the need for significant upfront investments. This approach enables businesses to incorporate AI functionalities efficiently and cost-effectively.

Building Community-Driven Solutions

The promise of AI and frugal innovation is not solely in the reduction of costs and the improvement of efficiency. It is about addressing the specific needs of underserved communities and creating sustainable, community-driven solutions. African American entrepreneurs have a deep understanding of the challenges their communities face, from education disparities to healthcare access, financial inclusion, and even food security. AI can help amplify this understanding by providing data-driven insights that lead to actionable strategies.

For example, data collection and analysis powered by AI can reveal patterns of underinvestment in certain neighborhoods or disparities in public service availability. Entrepreneurs can utilize these insights to advocate for changes, tailor their offerings to fill these gaps, or partner with local governments and organizations to provide meaningful interventions. Leveraging AI to analyze trends and adapt products ensures that solutions are not only efficient but also genuinely responsive to community needs.

Moreover, the power of community storytelling, amplified through AI, offers unique potential. AI-driven content creation tools can assist entrepreneurs in crafting narratives that resonate deeply with local audiences. Marketing campaigns can be personalized to reflect cultural touchpoints, ensuring that products and services do not just reach people but also connect with them in ways that inspire loyalty and advocacy.

Frugal innovation powered by AI offers a transformative opportunity for African American entrepreneurs to build impactful, sustainable businesses. By thoughtfully leveraging AI technologies, they can overcome traditional barriers, meet the needs of their communities, and contribute to broader economic growth and social advancement. The intersection of frugal innovation and AI provides not just a pathway for entrepreneurial success, but a chance to redefine economic opportunity and equity.

Embracing this approach requires a commitment to continuous learning, collaboration, and a willingness to rethink conventional methods of resource utilization. As technology continues to evolve, entrepreneurs who adopt AI-driven frugal innovation strategies will be well-positioned to lead and thrive in the digital age. By focusing on community-driven outcomes, ethical practices, and practical collaboration, African American entrepreneurs can harness AI not just as a tool for profit but as a force for lasting community impact and empowerment.

Inspiration Bite: Marques Brownlee

Marques Brownlee, known professionally as MKBHD, is a prominent tech reviewer and entrepreneur who leverages AI tools to create high-quality content. His work demonstrates frugal innovation in the digital age by utilizing accessible AI technologies to produce engaging and informative tech reviews. Brownlee's success highlights the potential of AI to enhance content creation and distribution, providing valuable insights into the practical applications of AI for entrepreneurs.

Source: https://theinfluencerforum.com/influencer-profiles/mkbhd/

Reflection Prompts

How can you leverage AI-driven frugal innovation to create affordable and accessible products or services that address the specific needs of the African American community?

What strategies can you employ to maximize limited resources through frugal innovation, and how can AI tools enhance these strategies to support your entrepreneurial goals?

How might embracing open-source AI technologies and collaborative partnerships contribute to frugal innovation in your business, and what impact could this have on scalability and sustainability?

Chapter 13

Looking Ahead

The best way to predict the future is to create it. – Peter Drucker

The dawn of the Artificial Intelligence (AI) era presents unparalleled opportunities and challenges for entrepreneurs worldwide. For African Americans, who have historically faced systemic barriers and inequities, the rise of AI offers a unique chance to redefine their role in the economy and society. This chapter explores the potential trajectories of AI development, the evolving global market, and the critical role that African American entrepreneurs can play in shaping a more inclusive and innovative future.

Community Catalyst: Envisioning Entrepreneurial Empowerment

In the near future, African American entrepreneur Maya Thompson launches a tech startup that uses advanced AI to empower small businesses in underserved communities. Her platform, called "Community Catalyst," employs machine learning algorithms to provide personalized business strategies, financial forecasting, and customer engagement tools tailored to each user's unique context. By leveraging AI to break down traditional barriers to market entry, such as limited access to capital and mentorship, Maya's venture enables a new generation of entrepreneurs to thrive. Her success not only transforms local economies but also sets a precedent for inclusive innovation, illustrating how AI can be a powerful catalyst for equitable growth and opportunity in African American communities.

Envisioning the Future: AI's Transformative Power

AI is set to revolutionize nearly every aspect of business and society. It has the potential to personalize services, automate decision-making, enhance productivity, and create entirely new categories of jobs. For African American entrepreneurs, these developments present opportunities to innovate in niche markets, address community-specific challenges, and develop solutions that promote equity and inclusion.

AI Empowered, 119–127

Published under exclusive licence by Emerald Publishing Limited
doi:10.1108/978-1-83662-816-320251014

AI is not just a tool; it is a transformative force that can unlock new possibilities in every sector. As AI continues to evolve, we will see more sophisticated and nuanced applications capable of transforming how we work, communicate, and even think. For African American entrepreneurs, this evolution represents an unprecedented opportunity to step into leadership roles in emerging industries, providing innovative solutions that can directly benefit their communities and society at large.

Several trends will shape the AI landscape for African American entrepreneurs. An increased focus on ethical AI, driven by concerns about bias in AI systems, highlights the need for diverse perspectives in AI development. African American entrepreneurs, with their deep understanding of the impact of bias and discrimination, are uniquely positioned to lead in the creation of ethical and inclusive AI solutions. This focus on ethical AI can serve as both a business opportunity and a way to influence the direction of technological development globally.

Furthermore, the rise of AI-as-a-Service will lower the barriers to entry for those with limited resources, allowing sophisticated AI capabilities to be leveraged without significant upfront investment. This trend will democratize access to powerful AI tools, enabling smaller enterprises to compete with larger, established companies. The growth of edge AI, where data processing occurs closer to the source, will open up new opportunities for applications in sectors such as healthcare, transportation, and manufacturing, empowering entrepreneurs to develop innovations that improve community well-being. By focusing on real-time data and localized processing, African American entrepreneurs can create solutions that directly address the unique challenges faced by their communities, such as access to quality healthcare and infrastructure improvements.

Additionally, the convergence of AI with other emerging technologies, such as blockchain, the Internet of Things (IoT), and quantum computing, offers fertile ground for African American entrepreneurs to create novel applications that transform industries. The interplay of these technologies could lead to breakthroughs in areas like secure data sharing, smart cities, and advanced manufacturing processes. By positioning themselves at the forefront of these convergences, African American entrepreneurs can not only capture economic value but also drive societal change in a direction that promotes inclusion and equity.

AI and the Global Market: Competing on a Global Stage

The market for AI solutions is increasingly global, presenting both opportunities and challenges for African American entrepreneurs. Digital platforms and cloud-based services have made accessing global markets easier than ever, providing African American entrepreneurs with the tools to compete on an international stage. However, success will require more than technological skill; it will require cultural intelligence, adaptability, and the ability to navigate different cultural and linguistic contexts.

The ability to adapt products and services for different regions of the world is key to success in the global AI marketplace. This requires a nuanced understanding of varying cultural preferences, market needs, and regulatory environments. African American entrepreneurs are uniquely positioned to offer culturally relevant AI solutions that address the needs of diverse populations, leveraging their insights into historically underserved communities. This global perspective can help distinguish their offerings from those of competitors.

International collaboration will also play a key role. Cross-border partnerships can provide African American entrepreneurs with access to new markets and diverse perspectives, making them better equipped to navigate the challenges of globalization. These collaborations may involve working with local partners who have in-depth knowledge of specific regional markets or partnering with organizations to access international funding and mentorship. The ability to work with remote teams, secure international funding, and understand global regulations will be essential for thriving in this environment.

Beyond traditional business opportunities, African American entrepreneurs can use AI as a tool for global social impact. AI can help tackle some of the world's most pressing problems, from poverty and inequality to healthcare and education. By positioning their companies to address global challenges, African American entrepreneurs can extend their influence beyond local markets and contribute to the greater good on a global scale.

Sustainability and AI: Building a Greener Future

AI has the potential to drive significant advancements in sustainability by optimizing energy consumption, reducing waste, improving climate modeling, and enabling sustainable farming practices. For African American entrepreneurs, this presents an opportunity to lead in developing AI-driven solutions that address environmental challenges, particularly those affecting underserved communities.

The intersection of AI and sustainability is ripe for innovation. African American entrepreneurs can leverage AI to create solutions that promote renewable energy use, improve efficiency in agriculture, and reduce the carbon footprint of transportation and logistics. By focusing on environmental challenges that disproportionately affect marginalized communities, such as air quality, water access, and food security, entrepreneurs can ensure that their AI innovations have a meaningful impact on those who need it most.

AI also enables more sustainable business models by facilitating the circular economy, supporting remote work, optimizing supply chains for minimal environmental impact, and helping businesses monitor and report their social and environmental impacts. African American entrepreneurs can create AI solutions that not only drive profitability but also promote environmental stewardship, contributing to a greener future for all. Imagine AI-driven tools that help small businesses track their environmental footprints or optimize their processes to reduce waste. These are innovations that could have a significant impact on both economic outcomes and environmental sustainability.

Ethical Considerations: Building Responsible AI

As AI becomes more integrated into society, ethical considerations are paramount. African American entrepreneurs have the opportunity to lead in the development of responsible AI practices that promote fairness and inclusion. Creating ethical AI requires diverse development teams, adherence to ethical guidelines, and continuous monitoring for unintended biases. Involving diverse stakeholders in the design and implementation of AI systems ensures that AI reflects the needs of all communities, not just a privileged few.

Responsible AI also means holding technology accountable for its social impact. African American entrepreneurs can work to ensure that AI systems are developed in ways that mitigate, rather than exacerbate, social inequalities. By embedding fairness, transparency, and accountability into AI models, entrepreneurs can set a precedent for the entire industry, showcasing how technology can be used to uplift marginalized communities. This kind of ethical leadership is crucial as AI systems become more involved in decision-making processes that affect people's lives, from hiring practices to healthcare diagnostics.

Anticipating Disruption: AI as a Catalyst for Change

AI's potential to disrupt industries and redefine markets is becoming increasingly clear. For African American entrepreneurs, this disruption brings both challenges and opportunities. Sectors like healthcare, finance, education, and agriculture are already being transformed by AI, offering new possibilities for innovation.

Disruption often sparks new business models, and those who can anticipate and adapt to these shifts are the ones who thrive. African American entrepreneurs can position themselves advantageously by adopting a proactive approach to change: say, by welcoming new technologies, learning about emerging trends, and staying attuned to shifts in consumer preferences. In healthcare, for example, AI tools can be used to create more equitable access to medical resources, while in education, AI can tailor learning experiences to meet the unique needs of underserved students. By identifying these areas of opportunity, African American entrepreneurs can establish themselves as early movers in new and rapidly growing sectors.

However, disruption also brings uncertainty. Entrepreneurs must anticipate changes in market dynamics and consumer behavior, adapting their strategies accordingly. This requires agility, a mindset of continuous learning, and the ability to evolve alongside technological advances. Embracing AI as a catalyst for change means not only using AI tools but also contributing to AI's development to ensure it reflects the needs of diverse communities. African American entrepreneurs must be ready to pivot their business models as technologies evolve, ensuring that they stay relevant in the face of rapid change.

The Global Opportunity: African American Entrepreneurs on the World Stage

The future of entrepreneurship is increasingly global, and AI allows even small businesses to access international markets. African American entrepreneurs can become leaders in addressing global challenges, from climate change to healthcare disparities, using AI to create scalable solutions that reach beyond their immediate communities.

Global thinking is critical in the AI era. For instance, AI-driven platforms could optimize supply chains, connecting small-scale farmers in Africa with markets in the United States, while language-processing tools could bridge cultural divides, enabling effective global collaborations. By thinking beyond local markets, African American entrepreneurs can establish themselves as global innovators, contributing to a more interconnected and equitable world economy. Addressing global issues through AI solutions also opens doors for funding from international organizations and impact investors who are eager to support initiatives with a strong social impact component.

Additionally, understanding global market trends and aligning with international standards can help African American entrepreneurs tap into new opportunities. Developing products that meet the diverse needs of global consumers, while ensuring compliance with international regulations, can enable entrepreneurs to expand their influence and impact. African American entrepreneurs have the potential to create a legacy that transcends national boundaries, inspiring future generations to think on a global scale.

Balancing Automation With Humanity

One of the central tensions in the AI era is balancing automation with humanity. While automation offers efficiency and scalability, it also raises concerns about job displacement and the loss of human connection. African American entrepreneurs are uniquely positioned to lead in creating AI solutions that augment, rather than replace, human experiences.

AI can be used to enhance personalized customer service, streamline repetitive tasks, and empower employees to focus on creative and relational aspects of their work. By emphasizing human-centered design, African American entrepreneurs can ensure that AI innovations align with values like empathy, fairness, and inclusion. AI should not be seen as a replacement for human labor but as a tool that enhances human capabilities. Entrepreneurs can develop AI systems that automate mundane tasks while keeping the human touch intact, ensuring that customers and employees alike feel valued and heard.

Moreover, African American entrepreneurs can be leaders in the movement to create jobs that require new kinds of skills, such as AI training, data management, and ethical auditing. By fostering AI systems that are used to empower rather than displace workers, these entrepreneurs can set an example for how AI and human labor can coexist harmoniously. This approach is not only ethically responsible but also economically advantageous, as it ensures a committed and engaged workforce that can grow alongside technological advancements.

Navigating Ethical Challenges in the AI Landscape

The rapid development of AI has outpaced the ethical frameworks needed to guide its implementation. Issues like algorithmic bias, data privacy, and accountability are pressing concerns, particularly for marginalized communities. African American entrepreneurs can take a proactive role by embedding ethical considerations into their AI solutions. That means creating systems that audit for bias, ensuring data privacy, and advocating for transparency in AI algorithms. By leading in responsible AI development, they can build trust and set a high standard for the industry.

Ethical AI is not merely a technical challenge; it is also a societal one. African American entrepreneurs can spearhead initiatives that bring together diverse stakeholders, including community groups, policymakers, and technologists, to ensure that AI systems are designed with equity in mind. Such collaborations are crucial in creating AI that serves everyone fairly, minimizing the risk of reinforcing existing inequalities. Advocacy and public education on AI ethics are also important areas where African American entrepreneurs can make significant contributions, raising awareness about the potential risks and benefits of AI technologies in society.

The Power of Storytelling in Shaping the Future

As AI reshapes the entrepreneurial landscape, storytelling becomes an essential tool for African American entrepreneurs. Stories have the power to inspire, educate, and drive change, helping entrepreneurs connect with investors, customers, and communities. By sharing their journeys, African American entrepreneurs can challenge stereotypes, highlight the impact of their innovations, and inspire the next generation of innovators. Social media, blogs, and podcasts offer powerful platforms for amplifying voices that have historically been underrepresented in the tech industry.

Effective storytelling can be the bridge between technology and humanity, making complex AI concepts accessible to the general public. African American entrepreneurs can use storytelling to demonstrate the tangible impact of their AI innovations: That is, how these technologies solve real-world problems and improve quality of life. By crafting compelling narratives, entrepreneurs can build strong brands, attract funding, and create a community of supporters who believe in their vision.

Moreover, storytelling is an important tool for advocacy. African American entrepreneurs can use their stories to highlight the importance of diversity in tech and the potential of AI to transform marginalized communities. By putting a human face on technology, they can build empathy and understanding, rallying support for more inclusive and ethical AI initiatives.

Investing in the Next Generation of Innovators

The road ahead is not just about today's entrepreneurs – it is about empowering the next generation. African American entrepreneurs can invest in education, mentorship, and community-building efforts that equip young people with the skills and confidence to lead in the AI era. Coding camps, startup incubators, and scholarships can create pathways for young African Americans into the tech industry. By fostering a culture of inclusiveness and innovation, entrepreneurs can ensure that their legacy extends far beyond their own ventures.

Mentorship programs are particularly impactful, as they provide young people with role models who can guide them through the challenges of entrepreneurship and technology development. African American entrepreneurs who have succeeded in AI can share their experiences, lessons learned, and insights to help the next generation avoid common pitfalls and accelerate their growth. Community-building initiatives, such as hackathons and workshops, can also provide young people with hands-on experience in AI, encouraging them to pursue careers in tech and innovation.

Investing in the next generation also means advocating for systemic changes in education. African American entrepreneurs can work with schools and policymakers to ensure that AI and tech education are accessible to all students, particularly those in underfunded and underserved communities. By championing science, technology, engineering and mathematics (STEM) education and working to close the digital divide, they can help create a pipeline of diverse talent ready to take on the challenges and opportunities of the AI era.

Collaborative Ecosystems: Driving Collective Progress

The challenges of the AI era are too complex to tackle alone. Collaborative ecosystems where entrepreneurs, researchers, policymakers, and community leaders work together are essential for driving progress. African American entrepreneurs can amplify their impact by participating in these ecosystems, accessing resources and expertise that would be difficult to obtain individually. Collaborative efforts can include joint ventures, industry consortia, or public–private partnerships, focusing on solving systemic challenges through AI.

These ecosystems provide not only access to resources but also a sense of community and shared purpose. By working together, stakeholders can pool their expertise and tackle challenges more effectively than they can alone. African American entrepreneurs, by participating in these collaborative environments, can influence the direction of AI development and ensure that their perspectives are included in decisions that shape the future. For instance, a consortium focused on ethical AI could benefit from the insights of diverse entrepreneurs who understand the real-world implications of bias and inequity.

Moreover, collaborative ecosystems encourage cross-disciplinary innovation. African American entrepreneurs can benefit from partnerships with researchers and technologists from other fields, sparking new ideas and innovative applications of AI. These collaborations can also open doors to new markets and investment opportunities, providing a broader platform for African American-led AI ventures to thrive.

Resilience in the Face of Change

The AI era is characterized by rapid and unpredictable changes, requiring resilience from entrepreneurs. African American entrepreneurs, who have historically navigated systemic barriers and economic uncertainties, are well-equipped to thrive in this evolving environment. Resilience means not only adapting to change but also advocating for reforms that create a more equitable playing field. By leveraging their experiences, African American entrepreneurs can build transformative businesses that push for systemic change.

Resilience is about more than bouncing back from setbacks; it is about transforming obstacles into opportunities. African American entrepreneurs can use their unique perspectives to identify unmet needs and create innovative solutions that others might overlook. This resilience is also reflected in the community networks that African American entrepreneurs often build and rely on networks that provide support, mentorship, and collaboration opportunities that are crucial for long-term success in the fast-paced AI industry.

By maintaining a mindset of growth and adaptability, African American entrepreneurs can navigate the uncertainties of the AI era, making strategic pivots when necessary and staying ahead of industry trends. They can also be advocates for change, pushing for systemic reforms that create a fairer, more inclusive landscape for all entrepreneurs. Through their resilience and determination, African American entrepreneurs can set a powerful example for others to follow, showing that it is possible to succeed and lead in the face of adversity.

A Vision for the Future: Redefining Success

The road ahead is about more than just breakthroughs in technology: it's an opportunity to rethink what it means to succeed. For African American entrepreneurs, thriving in the AI era involves more than financial growth; it's about creating businesses that reflect their values, strengthen their communities, and pave the way for a fairer world. This journey calls for a delicate balance between profit and purpose, using technology as a force for social good while inspiring others to dream big and take bold steps in entrepreneurship. By staying true to their vision and leading with integrity, African American entrepreneurs have the power to leave a meaningful mark on both AI and the future of entrepreneurship.

Redefining success also requires challenging the traditional measures of value. African American entrepreneurs have a unique chance to prove that success isn't just about profit margins but about the broader impact a business can make. Embedding social responsibility into the heart of their ventures can demonstrate that it's entirely possible to drive economic growth while fostering positive change. This shift in mindset can ripple through the tech industry, encouraging others to think more deeply about their impact and adopt a more inclusive and holistic approach to building businesses.

The potential for African American entrepreneurs in the AI space is vast. Tapping into that potential will take a united effort from all sides: entrepreneurs, educators, policymakers, and investors. We need to collectively push for better access to AI education and training for underrepresented groups, greater funding and resources for African American-led AI startups, diverse leadership in the field, and ethical policies that prioritize fairness and equity. Together, we can ensure that AI's future is not only groundbreaking but also inclusive, with African American innovators taking center stage in creating a brighter, more equitable future for everyone.

This journey is more than individual success stories. It's about building a legacy that inspires generations to come. By using AI as a tool for good, leading with integrity, and fostering collaboration, African American entrepreneurs can help build a world where technology serves everyone and innovation knows no limits.

Inspiration Bite: Nichol Bradford

Nichol Bradford is the Executive-in-Residence for AI + HI at the Society for Human Resource Management (SHRM), where she shapes global thinking on human–AI collaboration. She is also the co-founder and partner of Niremia Collective, an early-stage venture fund focused on human potential technologies. Bradford's work emphasizes the importance of ethical and empowering AI, advocating for the development of technologies that enhance human potential and well-being.

Source: https://www.shrm.org/about/bio/nichol-bradford

Reflection Prompts

What is your long-term vision for yourself or your business? How does AI fit into that vision?

What steps can you take today to prepare for the future challenges and opportunities of AI?

What legacy do you want to leave behind as an entrepreneur or innovator, and how can you start building it now?

Further Reading

Adam, H., Balagopalan, A., Alsentzer, E., Christia, F., & Ghassemi, M. (2022). Mitigating the impact of biased artificial intelligence in emergency decision-making. *Communication and Medicine*, *2*(1), 149.

Bonaparte, Y. (2024). *Innovation and entrepreneurship from the stone tool to artificial intelligence*. Cambridge Scholars Publishing.

de Souza Santos, R., Stuart-Verner, B., & De Magalhaes, C. V. (2023, May). Diversity in software engineering: A survey about scientists from underrepresented groups. In *2023 IEEE/ACM 16th international conference on cooperative and human aspects of software engineering (CHASE)* (pp. 161–166). IEEE.

Floyd, S. (2021). Assessing African American women engineers' workplace sentiment within the AI field. *The International Journal of Information, Diversity, & Inclusion (IJIDI)*, *5*(5).

Frost, S., Jung, Y., Rencher, M., & Batts, D. (2023). Re-centering race in emancipatory entrepreneurship: Black female tech founders, money, and meaning in a detroit-based incubator program. *Journal of Business Anthropology*, *12*(2), 114–137.

George, B., & Paul, J. (2020). *Digital transformation in business and society*. Springer International Publishing.

George, B., & Wooden, O. (2023). Managing the strategic transformation of higher education through artificial intelligence. *Administrative Sciences*, *13*(9), 196.

Jackson, M. C. (2021). Artificial intelligence & algorithmic bias: The issues with technology reflecting history & humans. *Journal of Business & Technology Law*, *16*, 299.

Jackson, F., D'Innocenzo, L., & Gefen, D. (2024). Embracing survivalist entrepreneurship: How African American men leverage business ownership out of economic necessity. *Business*, *4*(2), 177–195.

Joyce, K., Smith-Doerr, L., Alegria, S., Bell, S., Cruz, T., Hoffman, S. G., Noble, S. U., & Shestakofsky, B. (2021). Toward a sociology of artificial intelligence: A call for research on inequalities and structural change. *Socius*, *7*. https://doi.org/10.1177/2378023121999581

Keir, G., Hu, W., Filippi, C. G., Ellenbogen, L., & Woldenberg, R. (2023). Using artificial intelligence in medical school admissions screening to decrease inter-and intra-observer variability. *JAMIA Open*, *6*(1), ooad011.

Mao-Clark, X., Koh, Y., DeFranco, A., & Nakajima, R. (2024). African American style project pitches in business fundraising: Strategies for African American entrepreneurs. *International Journal of Hospitality Management*, *120*, 103783.

Mathis, M. S., Badewa, T. E., Obiarinze, R. N., Wilkinson, L. T., & Martin, C. A. (2021). A novel use of artificial intelligence to examine diversity and hospital performance. *Journal of Surgical Research*, *260*, 377–382.

Mengesha, Z., Heldreth, C., Lahav, M., Sublewski, J., & Tuennerman, E. (2021). "I don't think these devices are very culturally sensitive."—Impact of automated speech recognition errors on African Americans. *Frontiers in Artificial Intelligence*, *4*, 725911.

Mhlanga, D., & Dzingirai, M. (2023). Toward an inclusive industry 4.0: Social policy, economic growth, and development in Africa. In *The fourth industrial revolution in Africa: Exploring the development implications of smart technologies in Africa* (pp. 361–378). Springer Nature Switzerland.

Monroe-White, T., & McGee, E. (2024). Toward a race-conscious entrepreneurship education. *Entrepreneurship Education and Pedagogy*, *7*(2), 161–189.

Naudé, W. (2024). Destructive digital entrepreneurship. In *Handbook of research on entrepreneurship and conflict* (pp. 292–328). Edward Elgar Publishing.

Pearson, K., & Richardson, A. (2022). The language of liberation: A conversation with ruby sales. *Black History Bulletin*, *85*(2), 19–24.

Roshanaei, M. (2024). Towards best practices for mitigating artificial intelligence implicit bias in shaping diversity, inclusion and equity in higher education. *Education and Information Technologies*, 1–26.

Salas-Pilco, S. Z., Xiao, K., & Oshima, J. (2022). Artificial intelligence and new technologies in inclusive education for minority students: A systematic review. *Sustainability*, *14*(20), 13572.

Schelenz, L. (2022). Artificial intelligence between oppression and resistance: Black feminist perspectives on emerging technologies. In *Artificial intelligence and its discontents: Critiques from the social sciences and humanities* (pp. 225–249). Springer International Publishing.

Shahid, M. S., Hossain, M., Karami, M., & Anwar, T. (2023). Frugal entrepreneurship: A way to seize business opportunities for low-income customers. *Asia Pacific Journal of Management*, 1–31.

Singh, R. P., & Nurse, S. (2024). Addressing the racial Wealth gap and structural racism through increased black entrepreneurship: An entrepreneurial ecosystem perspective. *The Review of Black Political Economy*. https://doi.org/10.1177/00346446231226402

Walker, V. S. (1996). *Their highest potential: An African American school community in the segregated South*. University of North Carolina Press.

Wallace, R. (2021). The names have changed, but the game's the same': Artificial intelligence and racial policy in the USA. *AI and Ethics*, *1*(4), 389–394.

Williams, D. P. (2024). Disabling AI: Biases and values embedded in artificial intelligence. In *Handbook on the ethics of artificial intelligence* (pp. 246–261). Edward Elgar Publishing.

Williams, N. H. (2024). Artificial intelligence and algorithmic bias. In *Artificial intelligence and healthcare: The impact of algorithmic bias on health disparities* (pp. 1–18). Springer International Publishing.

Wooden, O. S. (2007). High school guidance counselors as reproductive forces in the lives of African American students: A study of a Georgia high school. In E. P. St John (Ed.), *Confronting education inequality: Reframing, building understanding, and making change, Readings on equal education* (Vol. 22, pp. 245–282). AMS Press.

Wooden, O. S. (2009). The African American tradition: A framework for increasing the educational outcomes of African Americans. In G. Robertson IV (Ed.), *Family Affair: Deconstructing the African American identity* (pp. 105–115). Agate Publishing.

Zhang, W., & Rodgers, S. (2023). Linking ethnicity targeting with artificial intelligence and data collection: Perceptions and behavioral responses of black consumers. *Journal of Current Issues and Research in Advertising*, *44*(3), 373–391.

Printed and bound by CPI Group (UK) Ltd, Croydon, CR0 4YY

11/06/2026

14897900-0001